HOLLYWOOD
BE THY

HOLLYWOOD
BE THY

RAY COMFORT

Bridge-Logos

Orlando, Florida 32822

Bridge-Logos

Orlando, FL 32822 USA

Hollywood Be Thy Name
by Ray Comfort

Printed in the United States of America.

Library of Congress Catalog Card Number: 2007929520
International Standard Book Number 978-0-88270-394-7

Scripture quotations in this book are from the *Evidence Bible* ("Comfortable King James Version").

Cover: Lynn Copeland, www.genesis-group.net
Back cover photo: Carol Scott, Covina CA, www.cj-studio.com
Front cover graphic: Dale Jackson

"For you have said in your heart, *I will ascend into heaven,*
I will exalt my throne above the stars of God...
I will be like the most High."
Isaiah 14:13-14

Contents

Hollywood's Secret

Who is your favorite movie star? Is it Thomas Mapother IV? Millions adore him. But do *you* like his movies? Do you like him as a person? Do you even know who he is? Here's a couple of clues to his identity: He's into Scientology. He starred in *Mission Impossible*. His Hollywood name may help you—Tom Cruise. Or do you like Issur Danilovich Demsky's movies? That was Kirk Douglas' name when he arrived in Hollywood. Bernard Schwartz became Tony Curtis, Joseph Levitch was transformed into Jerry Lewis, Nicolas Kim Coppola had his name changed to Nicolas Cage. Experts thought that the plain Jane name "Caryn Johnson" needed a lift, so she became Whoopie Goldberg. Charlie Sheen used to be called Carlos Irwin Estevez, Archibald Leach (understandably) was changed to Cary Grant. Christian Michael Leonard Hawkins became Christian Slater, Walter Willison took on the name Bruce Willis and Marion Michael Morrison became John Wayne[1].

Hollywood picked these unknowns out of the dirt and shaped them after its own image. It breathed into them the life of celebrity, then it enthroned itself as God, and millions bowed the knee to its revered name.

---

1 However, when you show up in Hollywood with bright eyes, a chiseled jaw, and biceps the size of a director's head, who cares if your name is Arnold Alois Schwarzenegger.

Each week the faithful believed in Hollywood and lined up to pay their tithes and fill the meeting-place they called a theater. Hollywood's name became hallowed, and the entire world sung her praises. Its kingdom had come. Its will was being done on earth, as it provided the daily bread of the massive entertainment industry. Its power and glory became so great that it eclipsed the personal light of its own stars.

For most of Hollywood's stars, it was more than just a name change. An image had to be created. Photos were taken, expensive clothes purchased, hairstyles changed. Restrictions were laid down as to what the actor could or couldn't say publicly, and contracts were signed. Each person became a carefully shaped golden calf ... a Hollywood graven image, a precious idol that would be looked up to and idolized by the world. The golden calf's sole purpose was to bring in the money at the box office.

In other words, the self-sufficient, independent tough guy, "I don't need God" image of John Wayne or Frank Sinatra we saw in the movies wasn't the true representation of who they were in real life.[2]

---

2 Some people just have a powerful screen presence and can become successful largely because the camera likes them. Another very famous actor known for his lack of acting skills was John Wayne. In *The Greatest Story Ever Told* (1965) Wayne had only one line as the Centurion: "Truly, this man was the son of God." The director, George Stevens, unimpressed by his wooden delivery, gave him some advice. "You're referring to the son of God here, Duke, you've got to deliver the line with awe." Wayne accepted the advice. On the next take he said, "Aw, truly this was the Son of God!"

As noted above, it isn't just about acting. The camera loves certain actors. "The camera just loves some people and it sure loves Marilyn (Monroe). Look at Bogart. Funny little man you wouldn't notice in a crowd, but on camera...! Look at Gary Cooper. Wonderfully tall and good looking, yes, but can't act for toffee and never even tries. Doesn't ever change his expression by a hair's breadth, and yet when you see him on camera, everyone with him seems to be overacting. Just born with the magic. And so is Marilyn. However confused or difficult she is in real life, for the camera she can do no wrong" (comment by Allan Snyder, American make-up artist). http://www.mtsu.edu/~socwork/frost/god/overview.htm

That was their on-screen image. But look to their own words about God and the Bible:

> "I've always had deep faith that there is a Supreme Being; there has to be. To me that's just a normal thing to have that kind of faith." [3] *–John Wayne*

> "I believe that God knows what each of us wants and needs. It's not necessary for us to make it to church on Sunday to reach Him. You can find Him anyplace." [4] *–Frank Sinatra*

Hollywood's money-making "immortals" were real people, individuals who had real hopes, dreams, and concerns about the future. And they had their own thoughts about God and the Bible. *But this was a side of Hollywood the public rarely saw.* We will look at the reason for this further on in this book.

The Elephant

As a young man it was a continual mystery to me as to why people were interested in God. My philosophy of life was one of pleasure. There didn't seem to be much else. Any serious thought about God didn't come into my mind. This was because I didn't think too deeply.

The issue of God is a mystery until we think seriously about life for a moment. There's a huge elephant in the humanity room, and he's going to eventually stomp on all of us. His name is "death." When we realize this, it makes sense for each of us to see if there is any way we can avoid being stomped on. That's why people usually become interested in God. Some of us are slower than others to get around to serious thought. But as those around them get stomped on and they bury their bodies, it dawns on them that they too have a problem. A big

---

3 *What Hollywood Believes*, Ray Comfort, (p. 66).
4 *What Hollywood Believes*, Ray Comfort, (p. 82).

one. It's an issue everyone with a brain thinks about, but few people talk about.

However, Kirk Cameron and I bring up the issue on our television and radio programs. We ask people what they think happens after someone dies, and we find that it's an issue that most people are more than willing to talk about, if they are asked.

The common answer is, "I don't know." Asked if they think about the issue, it's common to hear, "All the time."

When Barbara Walters[5] was asked about the matter of the afterlife, she said, "I think everybody wonders, is there life after death? Recently, when I've been at dinners, I've gone around the table and said, "How many of you believe in life after death?" It's so interesting to hear your friends' answers, because sometimes they're very surprising. Sometimes you'll find that husbands and wives disagree.

> "I think everybody wonders, is there life after death?"
> –Barbara Walters

"What I feel more and more is how important it is to live your life in a better way, and not to worry about it," Walters said. "What happens will happen."

When she was asked if there was a heaven, would she expect that she would go there, she answered, "I have no idea." She didn't have any sort of religious upbringing, saying once again, " … I really do believe that the most important thing is the way you live your life on earth. But I think it's enormously comforting to believe that you're going to see your loved ones."[6]

Defuse the Fuse

Before we look closely at Hollywood, let me lay an important foundation so that what I have to say about it will make sense. In early February of 2007, one man I asked

---

5 American journalist who was a regular fixture on morning television shows (*Today* and *The View*), evening news magazine (*20/20*), and on *The ABC Evening News*, as the first female evening news anchor.

6 http://www.beliefnet.com/story/181/story_18118_1.html

about the afterlife didn't react well to my question. He retorted "Why do you ask?" I tried to defuse the fuse I had lit by casually saying, "Oh, I was just wondering. We have a television program in which we ask that question and most people are more than willing to talk about it," and quickly changing the subject. Later on the man apologized and began asking me some very thought-provoking questions, such as "Why were we created?" I told him that we were created to bring God glory. His reaction was predictable. He said, "He must be the ultimate egotist." It was predictable because he was what the Bible calls a "natural" man, and it says that the natural man thinks that the things of God are foolish.[7]

I explained that God does seem like the ultimate egotist, if you look at it from a "natural" perspective. But He is nothing like us. He is without sinful pride. Any honor, praise or glory spoken of is justly due to Him.

Jesus of Nazareth also seems to be the ultimate egotist. He told His disciples that their eyes and ears were blessed because they were seeing and hearing Him.[8] He was talking about *Himself*. In another portion of the Scriptures He speaks of Himself as being meek and lowly of heart. He even told His disciples that if the crowds didn't call out in praise to Him, the stones would.[9]

That is amazing—that any human being would talk like that. However, the issue becomes even more amazing when we realize who the Bible says this Person was. We are told that this Man Jesus was the Creator—the One who made all things, *and the One who is the essence of and the source of life itself.*

One of His disciples wrote about this when he spoke of actually physically touching Jesus when he was with Him. [10]

---

7 See 1 Corinthians 2:14

8 See Matthew 13:16-17.

9 See Luke 19:40

10 "That which was from the beginning, which we have heard, which we have seen with our eyes, which we have looked upon, and our hands have handled, of the Word of life; (For the life was manifested, and we have seen

If that was true (that He was the source of life in human form), then everything He said about His hearers being "blessed" was true. Nothing came from a puffed up human ego. He was speaking *absolute* truth.

The Actual Painter

I also said to my friend, "Imagine you are standing looking with awe at what you think is the most beautiful painting ever painted. It is breathtaking beyond words. As you gaze at its incredibly majesty, its amazing wonder, you are told that the actual painter is standing beside you. What are you going to do? Do you ignore him? Of course not. You cannot help yourself. Words spill from your excited lips, and you say, 'Did you paint that? It is absolutely magnificent. You are a *wonderful* artist!' You give him due honor. You give him appropriate praise. Anything less than that would be a sin.

"Think about it. God painted every breathtaking sunrise, every massive snow-capped mountain, He made the deep blue seas with their teeming life, and the magnificent clouds that pour their water on the thirsty earth. He painted creation with vibrant colors. He filled the canvas of life with amazing animals, with gorgeous flowers, brightly colored birds and tall green oxygen-exhaling trees. The Bible uses personification when speaking of God, saying that trees of the field clap their hands, the hills sing, the stones cry out in praise to Him because of who He is and what He has done. The trees lift their branches in worship to Him. The flowers blossom to His glory, and the birds sing His wonderful praises … and He is standing right beside you.

"Imagine now that you are back looking at the incredible painting. There is a man beside you who is raving about it as much as you did. But when he finds out that the person next to him is the actual painter, he spits on him, cusses him out, and for some unknown reason adamantly denies that the

---

it, and bear witness, and show to you that eternal life, which was with the Father, and was manifested to us;)" (1 John 1:1-2).

painting even had a painter. He says the unthinkable. He says it happened by accident."

That's what much of this world does.[11] The Creator is right beside them and they blaspheme His name, refuse to give Him due praise for who He is and what He has done, or thanksgiving for the gift of life—and some of them do the unthinkable. They deny His existence and say that the entire miracle of creation was an accident.

Why would they do that? The Bible tells us that it is because of His moral government.[12] He demands moral responsibility, and that especially flies in the face of Hollywood, because most of the entertainment industry is made up of "natural" men and women, who live their lives in search of nothing but pleasure, rather than God.

John Wayne and Filthy Minds

Hollywood movies reveal that it disdains God. The average Hollywood production uses the name of "God" and "Jesus Christ" more than the average sermon. Modern movies are *filled* with blasphemy. Haven't they noticed that "God" and "Jesus" aren't four-lettered words?

John Wayne was a major star from the 1940s to the 1970s and became famous for his distinctive voice and walk. He featured heavily in Westerns and World War II epics, but he also made a wide range of films from various genres, biographies, romantic comedies, police dramas, and more. He epitomized a rugged individualistic masculinity and has become an enduring American icon. In 1999, the American Film Institute named Wayne among "the greatest male stars of all time."

---

11 "For the invisible things of him from the creation of the world are clearly seen, being understood by the things that are made, even his eternal power and Godhead; so that they are without excuse: Because that, when they knew God, they glorified him not as God, neither were thankful; but became vain in their imaginations, and their foolish heart was darkened" (Romans 1:20,21).

12 See Romans 8:7

But this icon of masculinity deplored the use of profanity in the movies. He believed that it came from the filmmaker's idea of what adolescents liked to see. He rejected the notion that "foul language is a sign of machismo," and the feeling that "by using four-letter words they make somebody manly or sophisticated." He was against "filthy minds, filthy words, and filthy thoughts in films," regarding movies as "a universal instrument at once entertaining people and encouraging them to work toward a better world, a freer world." John Wayne had strong ideas about preserving "morality standards" and making films with a positive point of view.[13]

The Hollywood image of John Wayne was nothing like John Wayne the man.

---

13 http://www.adherents.com/people/pw/John_Wayne.html

Big Stars

Not too many people know the history of Hollywood. Even fewer know an ironic offer that was made to settlers:

In 1887, long before the film industry was a reality in Hollywood, let alone a going concern, a Kansas real estate tycoon named Horace Henderson Wilcox began mapping out the streets of a town built especially for stolid Midwesterners, sick of ice and snow. Being pious Midwesterners themselves, they banned saloons and offered land gratis to any church willing to locate there. The Wilcoxes' embryonic community was nestled at the foot of a ridge of gentle hills which sheltered the farms from the brutal desert winds, twelve miles from the Pacific Ocean. It was an idyllic setting, and fittingly, Wilcox's homesick wife named the nascent settlement Hollywood after the country place of a family friend. [1]

Who would have believed it? Free land was offered to any church that was willing to locate there. It's not too much of an exaggeration to say that nowadays, Hollywood would give free land to any Christian church who would locate *elsewhere*.

America may not be anti-God, but for some reason Hollywood is, and celebrities who are prepared to live out their Christian convictions will more than likely be blacklisted, unless they are too big to touch.

---

1 http://www.bookrags.com/research/hollywood-sjpc-02/

Jane Russell[2] said, "The trouble today in Hollywood is that the kids that try to share their faith overtly just don't get work, unless they're already a big star."[3]

Jim Carrey is big enough to speak about his spirituality without repercussions (he's one of a handful of actors who commands $25 million a picture). Back in November of 2004, in a rare interview he appeared on "60 Minutes" on CBS, where he candidly spoke to Steve Croft:

> "I'm a Buddhist, I'm a Muslim, I'm a Christian."
> –Jim Carrey

"I was on Prozac for a long time," he tells Kroft. "It may have helped me out of a jam for a little bit, but people stay on it forever." Then he describes being on the medication as not taking away the illness' peaks and valleys, only softening them. "There are peaks, there are valleys, but they're all kind of carved and smoothed out ... It feels like a low level of despair you live in where you're not getting any answers but you're living okay and you can smile at the office," he says. "You know, I had to get off at a certain point because I realized that ... everything is okay."

Carrey takes nothing now. "I rarely drink coffee. I am very serious about no alcohol, no drugs," he says, "Life is too beautiful."

During the interview at his home, he invited 60 Minutes cameras to one of his most beautiful and private spots, his "center of the universe," where he goes to escape the world and where he tells Kroft his feelings about God. "This is where I hang out with Buddha, Krishna ... all those guys," says Carrey about a lean-to adorned with candles and a bed built high on his hillside property in Brentwood, California.

"I'm a Buddhist, I'm a Muslim, I'm a Christian. I'm whatever you want me to be ... it all comes down to the

---

2 In 1940, Jane Russell was signed to a seven-year contract by millionaire Howard Hughes and made her motion picture debut in *The Outlaw* (1943), a story about Billy the Kid. She went on to star in more than 20 motion pictures.

3 http://www.mediawisefamily.com/syw/i-russell.html

same thing," he tells Kroft. Carrey says he believes they are all the same God and it is this conviction and spirituality that make him happy.[4]

It's All the Same

Islam, Christianity, Hinduism and Buddhism … they are the four main religions. But experts tell us that there are nineteen major world religious groupings in the world that are subdivided into a total of about 10,000 distinct religions. Then, within Christianity, there are approximately 34,000 separate groups (denominations, sects, individual unaffiliated churches, etc.) in the world.[5]

With all these often opposing beliefs, what are we supposed to believe happens when someone dies? Some believe in annihilation, some in a form of energy-less existence, then there's purgatory, Heaven or Paradise, the existence of Hell, limbo, reincarnation, transmigration of the soul, nirvana, and so on.

So, is our salvation like a spiritual buffet? Do we walk along life's path with our plate held in front of us and pick and choose whatever we fancy? Many in Hollywood do just that. That includes Dennis Quaid who mixes a little Hinduism with his Christianity:[6]

"I grew up Baptist. I'm a Christian, and I've been baptized twice: once when I was nine years old, and then

4 http://www.cbsnews.com/stories/2004/11/18/60minutes/main656547.shtml

5 http://www.religioustolerance.org/reltrue.htm

6 Best Known As: Star of *Frequency* and *The Rookie*. His most prominent role early in his career was that of astronaut Gordon Cooper in the 1983 film *The Right Stuff*. He has appeared on screen as a stranded astronaut in *Enemy Mine* (1985); as Jerry Lee Lewis in *Great Balls of Fire!* (1989, with Winona Ryder); as Doc Holliday in the western feature *Wyatt Earp* (1994, starring Kevin Costner); in *The Parent Trap* (1998); in *Frequency* (2000); as a shady lawyer in *Traffic* (2000); as pitcher Jim Morris in the 2002 biopic *The Rookie*; in *Far From Heaven* (2002); as Sam Houston in *The Alamo* (2004); in *The Day After Tomorrow* (2004); *Yours, Mine and Ours* (2005).

about five years ago, I got re-baptized—by a friend of mine, John Meyrick, a Baptist minister—in India, in the Ganges River.

"I've always been a seeker, and I think everyone needs to have a spiritual life. Along with that comes spiritual growth, and my faith is what's gotten me through tough times in my life. And so, besides being Christian, I've been all around the world, and I've always been interested in other religions as well. I've read the Koran twice, and I've read the Bhagavad Gita and the Dama Pata. I've asked people in my travels what they believe in, and why, and it makes for great discussions, actually.

> "I've read the
> *Koran* twice,
> and I've read the
> *Bhagavad Gita* and
> the *Dama Pata.*"
> –Dennis Quaid

"I've attended church throughout my life, as well as studied and explored other religions as well. I've been to India several times, and I discovered meditation in my life, which I still practice, and which I don't find conflicts with Christianity. In fact, Jesus himself meditated and told us to go off and be alone with our thoughts, and to know God. God is within you, and I think that's what meditation is, is to connect with God within yourself." [7]

In another interview he added:

"I grew up Baptist and still go to church. I myself have explored other religions, because I want to know what it is that makes other people tick. I find we're all talking about the same thing, really—it's all God. I went around the world three times and made it a point to ask people what it is that they believe and why. What I find is that we're all human beings and that it's all very similar, what we believe. At the bottom, there's really not that much difference between Christians and Muslims and Hindus and Buddhists. We all worship God." [8]

---

7 http://www.christianitytoday.com/movies/interviews/dennisquaid.html
8 http://www.beliefnet.com/story/178/story_17846_1.html

Goldie Hawn[9] mixed in a little Islam, Buddhism, Hinduism, Shamanism and Judaism with her Christianity:

> "The interesting part of my spiritual life is studying as much as you can. Islam and Buddhism and Hinduism and Shamanism and Judaism, Christianity—you try to learn what the precepts are, what the religion is, and ultimately, it's based in the same thought, it's based in the same outcome…"[10]

Are Jim Carrey, Goldie Hawn and Dennis Quaid right? Do we all worship the same God? Does it "all comes down to the same thing"? That would certainly clear the air of the confusion. This is another issue we will look at later on in this book.

A Godless Industry

A super nova is a star that suddenly increases dramatically in brightness and then fades to its original luminosity over a short period of months or years. Jim Carrey is a super nova— a super star, but most of his contemporaries don't have too much shine at all. They are at the mercy of executives, and the decision-makers especially don't like it when Christians try to live out their faith in Hollywood. This is because there's more than the natural disdain that Hollywood has for the gospel. There are financial reasons to blacklist Christians.

An actor who has a genuine faith in Jesus Christ will live his life accordingly. He will not take his clothes off and jump into bed with a woman, even if it is "just a movie." He will *strive* to be blameless. So when a sexually explicit script comes his way, he will either turn it down or seek to make changes,

---

9 Goldie Hawn won an Oscar for her major movie debut, a supporting role in *Cactus Flower* (1969, with Walter Matthau). She's been in movies from comedies to serious roles. She is probably best known for the 1980 comedy *Private Benjamin*.

10 http://www.beliefnet.com/story/172/story_17266_2.html

and few script writers want actors making changes to their script. Any holdup in production can be very expensive, so the actor quickly becomes known as a troublemaker.

Why then doesn't Hollywood simply begin producing wholesome movies with a deep spiritual theme, if that's what mainstream America wants? Why are they so anti-God[11]? The answer is simple. Those in the entertainment industry are typically self-confident and talented people, many of whom admit to having rather large egos. They are proud of who they are and what they have achieved. They want to be in front of the camera—in the spotlight. They are not the type of people who gravitate toward the selfless humility of Christianity. Rather, they are offended by the principles of a religion that talks of modesty, of childlike faith, of a babe in a manger, and of a king on a donkey. Any talk of the reality of personal sin and the need for God's forgiveness in Christ is anathema. Consequently, we have a nucleus of people in the entertainment business whose life's philosophy is godless, and this is clearly reflected in their God-less industry.

In a speech where he spoke of why there is a disconnection between Hollywood and America, "Wheel of Fortune" host Pat Sajak[12] said:

> "Former *CBS* newsman Bernard Goldberg has written a best-selling book called *Bias*, in which he maintains that the real problem with the media is not a bias based on liberal vs. conservative or Republican vs. Democrat. It is a bias based on the sameness of worldview caused by social, intellectual,

---

11 A February 2004 Fox News-Opinion Dynamics poll asked: "In general, do you think Hollywood moviemakers share your values or not?" Thirteen percent said yes, but an overwhelming 70 percent said no. Fox News also asked, "Do you think Hollywood is in touch with the life of the average American or is Hollywood out of touch with most Americans?" Nineteen percent said Hollywood's in touch; 72 percent, out of touch." http://www.mediaresearch.org/

12 Host of *Wheel of Fortune*, television production company owner, radio station owner (Annapolis, MD), music publisher, board member of the American Cinema Foundation

educational and professional inbreeding. These are folks who travel in the same circles, go to the same parties, talk to the same people, compare their ideas, and develop a standard view on issues that makes any deviation from them seem somehow marginal, or even weird.

"How can you write about people fairly if they seem so out of touch with what you are used to in your everyday life? That might help explain why religion is rarely depicted as a natural part of life in the average sitcom or drama series, despite the fact that tens of millions of Americans say that it is important to them."[13]

In other words a godless Hollywood lives in its own self-affirming monastery without walls. Casting director Reuben Cannon said, "Hollywood does not understand the people who live between New York and California."

Patricia Heaton[14] said, "People look at the stuff that comes out of Hollywood and think, 'Who are the people making this garbage? They couldn't possibly have any connection to God.'"

Speaking of when he first arrived in Hollywood at the age of nineteen, Jim Carrey said, "It was very traumatic. I spent the first night in a seedy motel on Sunset Boulevard." He was reading *The Late Great Planet Earth,* and it contained a biblical reference he wasn't familiar with, and as his room contained no Bible, he went to ask the manager for one. He says, "I said, 'Excuse me, sir, there's no Bible in my room.' And the manager said, 'Son, there isn't an entire Bible in the whole of Hollywood.'" [15]

---

13 http://www.christiananswers.net/spotlight/movies/discernment/hollywood-america.html

14 Patricia Heaton (born March 4, 1958 in Bay Village, Ohio) is an Emmy Award-winning actress. She is best known for playing lead character and Ray Barone's wife Debra Barone on the CBS television sitcom *Everybody Loves Raymond.*

15 http://www.cinema.com/news/item/1136/jim-carreys-godless-hollywood-experience.phtml

Look at the Darkness

Hollywood loves the darkness and they hate the light. That's normal for the entire human race. [16] But look at the *depth* of Hollywood's darkness[17]:

> A survey conducted among the 104 top television writers and executives found only 49 percent consider adultery to be wrong. That means 51 percent believe adultery is morally right. Meanwhile 85 percent of the rest of America believes adultery is wrong. When asked about their religious affiliations, 45 percent of Hollywood executives said they had none, while the number of Americans who had no religious affiliation was a mere 4 percent. [18]

Humanity drinks iniquity "like water," and Hollywood has a bottomless and contaminated lake to keep the supply flowing. Back in 1999 Michael Ellison wrote:

> "Movies with a 'G' (unrestricted) certificate produce a 78 percent greater return on investment than those with an 'R' (over 17s only) rating, say the data commissioned from Paul Kagan Associates, who examined the performance of the 2,380 films released in the United States on more than 800 screens in the 10 years to 1997. Only 75 of them went out with a 'G' rating.
>
> "The foundation [The Dove Foundation (www.dove. org)] claims that the findings contradict filmmakers who believe their work must be full of 'naked bodies, exploding heads and filthy language' if it is to make money."
>
> "Hollywood really doesn't make movies for the general public," Dick Rolfe, chief executive officer of The Dove Foundation, said yesterday.

---

16   See John 3:19-20.

17   "The light of the body is the eye: if therefore your eye is single, your whole body shall be full of light. But if your eye is evil, your whole body shall be full of darkness. If therefore the light that is in you is darkness, how great is that darkness!" (Matthew 6:22-23).

18   *Newsweek*, July 1992, www.geocities.com/RegnevaT/pp/television.htm

"They make movies to satisfy their own ego. Hollywood lives off cash flow and as long as there's enough cash to feed the monster the industry is satisfied." Gross profits for G-rated films in the review averaged $94 million against $11 million for the R-rated films and about $26 million for those with a 'PG' —parental guidance—rating.[19]

A 2003 study revealed:

Negativity toward religion grew steadily with each passing hour of prime time. During the 7 p.m. hour, religious content was negative 16.9 percent of the time. In the 8 p.m. hour, 20.8 percent of instances were negative. In the 9 p.m. hour, 27.5 percent of instances were negative, and in the 10 p.m. hour, 28.2 percent were negative.

These findings lend credibility to the idea that Hollywood accepts spirituality but shies away from endorsing, or even tolerating, organized religion.[20]

Michael Medved, author of *Hollywood vs. America*, said, "Defenders of the tired, dysfunctional Hollywood *status quo* can no longer manipulate figures or plead ignorance to justify the misguided emphasis on entertainment drenched with violence, graphic sex and foul language." But Len Klady, film industry analyst for the trade magazine *Variety*, said: "Oh please, spare us Michael Medved. This whole argument is specious. If people don't want to see a movie it doesn't matter how it's classified."

He then went on to quote statistics that revealed that a wholesome family movie that was released at the same time as a smut movie was a flop, while the dirt brought in millions.

"The majority like it, so it must be good" doesn't work when it comes to God. If our entire nation loved a movie

---

19 http://www.dove.org/news/london_guardian.htm
20 http://www.crosswalk.com/1301813/

that was filled with adultery and blasphemy, it is still wrong because it is *God*, not humanity, who sets the standard.

The Power of Celebrity

I was once interviewing a gentleman about celebrities and spirituality, and as an appreciation for those who were willing to do an interview I would give them a complimentary copy of *What Hollywood Believes*. At the conclusion I said, "I have a free book for you." The man said, "I don't want it. I don't like reading." I said, "You will want this one." He replied, "No, I won't." I mumbled, "Yes, you will." Again, he adamantly responded that he didn't want it. I handed it to him anyway and said, "It's the spiritual beliefs of 124 big name celebrities." He looked at the cover, said, "*Kevin Costner!*" and walked off clutching the book. Ten minutes later he returned and said, "Hey, thanks for the book!"

Celebrity is *very* powerful. Take the time to check out prime time TV and see what holds the interest of the world. You will find reruns of "Hollywood Squares," "Hollywood Justice," "Hollywood HD," "Access Hollywood," "Celebrity Blackjack," "Entertainment Tonight," "Extra," and "The Insider," just to name a few. All those programs major on celebrities—what they think, do, say, what they are wearing, what they are working on, what they are planning, and who is going with whom (think of why you showed interest in this book). Almost all of us are interested in the lives of the famous—particularly those in Hollywood. In the next chapter, we will look further at what some of them believe.

The Baby and the Bathwater

The human mind is amazing. It has the ability to do brilliant things. A man can train his mind to direct every part of his body to focus on walking a narrow tightrope across Niagara Falls. Blindfolded. The human mind can create music, machines, computers, cameras, and a mass of other incredible things, and yet it can be so self deceptive. It can look at this amazing creation and deny that it was created and pat itself on the back as intelligent for doing so.

Seth Green[1] is a professing atheist. He said, "God is, to me, [is] pretty much an idea. God is, to me, [is] pretty much a myth created over time to deny the idea that we're all responsible for our own actions." [2]

Notice the use of the words "to me." It reveals the assumption that realities are subjective. But no matter how many "to me's" we may introduce into the equation of God, the reality of His existence doesn't change. To me, the moon may be made of cheese, but my *perception* is irrelevant when it comes to reality.

1 Seth Green was born in Philadelphia, PA, in 1974. He began acting at the age of six. His uncle was a casting director and was able to help him land jobs on television and commercials. He appeared briefly in *Hotel New Hampshire*, with Rob Lowe. His big break came in *Can't Buy Me Love*.

2 http://www.quinnell.us/religion/famous/eh.html

Our Reps

One of the great problems for modern Christianity is its representatives. We see half naked females thank the Lord for the success of their movies or music, religious systems that are filled with pedophiles, and preachers who unashamedly line their pockets with easy money, and each one says that he or she represents God.

Alan Alda[3] is just one of millions who have (justifiably) become disillusioned with the traditional church as he sees it:

> "After our first baby came [late 1950s], I abandoned the formalities of the Catholic church. Although I had practiced my religion meticulously as I had been taught from infancy to do, I found that I now had questions that couldn't be answered by the church and could no longer accept concepts that I had always taken for granted simply because I was told to do so."

> "I used to be a Catholic," Alan told *Ms.* magazine. He left the church, he says, "because I object to conversion by concussion. If you don't agree with what they teach, you get clobbered over the head until you do. All that does is change the shape of the head."[4]

Susan Sarandon is another celebrity who had a problem with the Catholic church. She said:

> "My problem with the [Catholic] Church—I was brought up Catholic—was that Jesus' life was a very hands-on spirituality. It wasn't about excluding people. It was exactly the opposite. He was a shepherd to those people

---

3   Alan Alda (born Alfonso Joseph D'Abruzzo on January 28, 1936) is an Oscar-nominated and Emmy Award-winning American actor, writer, director and sometime political activist. He is most famous for his role as Hawkeye Pierce in the television series *M*A*S*H*. In the 1970s and 1980s he was viewed as the archetypal "sensitive male," though in recent years he has appeared in roles that counter that image.

4   http://www.adherents.com/people/pa/Alan_Alda.html

who had been excluded already from the mainstream and who were needy.

"I always envisioned the Church more as they do in some Latin American countries, where they're involved in the plight of the poor and in justice—all those things that politicize you once you start to open your eyes.

"Any religion that is so black and white—to me, that's like fanaticism. Religion is not black and white. It's much more complicated. Spirituality is much bigger than that. God is much bigger than that. I don't believe in a wrathful God. I believe he's much more forgiving and inclusive than some religions. The things that are done in her name or his name are horrible."[5]

However, Martin Scorsese doesn't seemed to be too disillusioned. He says of his beliefs, "I'm a lapsed Catholic. But I am Roman Catholic—there's no way out of it."[6] GodAmongDirectors.com says of him: "Martin Scorsese was born in Flushing, New York. Through most of his life, his chosen career goal was to be a priest. However, he later had a change of heart, and decided instead to become a filmmaker... In 1976, Scorsese directed the film for which he is probably most famous for, the ultra-violent *Taxi Driver* which drew controversy after it inspired John Hinckley's assassination attempt on President Ronald Reagan in 1981."[7]

Producer Martin Scorsese ... has drawn heavily on his Catholic boyhood for film inspiration. He notes: "The church and the movie house both are places for people to come together and share a common experience. I believe there is spirituality in films, even if it's not one that can supplant faith. I have found over the years that many films address themselves to the spiritual side of man's nature,

---

5　http://www.beliefnet.com/story/170/story_17020_4.html

6　*After Image: The Incredible Catholic Imagination of Six Catholic American Filmmakers*, Robert A. Blake, Loyola Press, 2000, p. 25

7　http://www.godamongdirectors.com/scorsese/index.shtml

from Griffith's *Intolerance* (1916) to John Ford's *The Grapes of Wrath* (1940) to Hitchcock's *Vertigo* (1958) to Kubrick's *2001* (1968) and so many more . . . It's as if movies answer an ancient quest for the common unconscious. To fulfill a spiritual need that people have to share a common memory."[8]

The Difference

For those who are unaware of the fact, there are two main divisions of traditional Christianity—the Roman Catholic and the Protestant Church. The Protestant Church is called *protestant* because it "protested" against Catholicism back in the early 1500s:

> Without quite intending to, Martin Luther changed the course of Christianity and Western history. His 1517 complaint against specific abuses in the Roman Catholic church—a document now known as the 95 Theses—sparked the explosive Protestant Reformation that swept Europe for the rest of the century. Born to a Roman Catholic family (his father was a copper miner), Luther graduated from the University of Erfurt in 1505 but abandoned his legal studies to enter a monastery devoted to St. Augustine. He was ordained to the priesthood in 1507 and by 1512 was a doctor of theology and a Bible professor at the University of Wittenberg. Luther was a gifted preacher but his theology began to clash with that of the Catholic church: he wrote that salvation came not by any human work but by absolute faith in God's promise of forgiveness on account of Jesus Christ. Luther didn't anticipate the uproar touched off by the 95 Theses he sent to a bishop and archbishop to protest "indulgences" being sold by the Catholic hierarchy. His controversial beliefs earned him excommunication from the church, but he pressed on with many new followers. Luther produced the first reader-friendly German translation of the Bible and developed a new form of Christian worship that

8 Lynn Haney, *Gregory Peck: A Charmed Life*, Carroll & Graf Publishers: New York, NY (2003), pages 50-51.

emphasized preaching and popular hymns, permitted the clergy to marry, and honored ordinary life in the world as a field for God's service.[9]

He made reference to "indulgences" 35 times in his Theses. These were monetary payments given by the pope for the forgiveness of sins. He said, "Thus those indulgence preachers are in error who say that a man is absolved from every penalty and saved by papal Indulgences."[10]

Martin Luther became the first to "protest" against what he saw as the errors of the Roman church, and thus he became the father of the Protestant church.

The Catholic Church traces its history right back to the Church of the first century, founded by Jesus Christ, and maintains that the true Church is built on Peter, the first pope. However, the Protestant church protests this, pointing to the contradicting testimony of the Scriptures, specifically where the New Testament says that Peter himself denied this fact, maintaining that Jesus Christ is the Rock and Chief Cornerstone of the Church.[11]

The Protestant Church says that Catholicism actually had a later beginning, when in the fourth century Constantine unified the Roman Empire by merging paganism with Christianity. Declaring himself Vicar of Christ, he elevated "converts" to positions of influence and authority. These professing Christians brought their pagan rites, their gods, and their goddesses into the church. In time, church councils began to exalt their traditions above Scripture and condemn their opponents, and many devout men were labeled heretics

---

9 http://www.answers.com/topic/martin-luther

10 http://www.fordham.edu/halsall/source/luther95.txt

11 "Wherefore also it is contained in the scripture, Behold, I lay in Zion a chief corner stone, elect, precious: and he that believeth on him shall not be confounded. Unto you therefore which believe he is precious: but unto them which be disobedient, the stone which the builders disallowed, the same is made the head of the corner" (1 Peter 2:6-8).

and persecuted for defending the Bible's authority. (Traditions are based on the words of men. Scripture is the Word of the Living God. When the two disagree, the Word of God must have immediate precedent. There is no contest).

By the twelfth century the Roman Catholic church had become the world's most powerful institution. It used its huge religious and political power to set up and depose of kings and queens. It taxed people and confiscated property and became the richest institution on earth. The pope offered crusading armies riches and eternal bliss to kill Muslims, those they considered "heretics," and anyone who rejected papal supremacy. Beginning in 1092 "the Crusades" began. These were a series of military campaigns in the Holy Land and elsewhere, sanctioned by the Pope.

> After pronouncing a solemn vow, each warrior received a cross from the hands of the pope or his legates, and was thenceforth considered a soldier of the [Catholic] Church. Crusaders were also granted indulgences and temporal privileges, such as exemption from civil jurisdiction, inviolability of persons or lands, etc. *The Catholic Encyclopedia*

Beginning around 1184, the Catholic church began what is called the "Inquisition." This was aimed at securing religious and doctrinal unity within the church, and sometimes persecution of alleged heretics. A conviction of heresy, seen as treason against Christendom, involved penalties ranging from a fine to a sentence of capital punishment such as burning at the stake administered by the state.

> In the second half of the twelfth century, however, heresy … spread in truly alarming fashion, and not only menaced the Church's existence, but undermined the very foundations of Christian society. In opposition to this propaganda there grew up a kind of prescriptive law … which visited heresy with death by the flames. Duke Philip of Flanders, aided

by William of the White Hand, Archbishop of Reims, was particularly severe towards heretics. They caused many citizens in their domains ... to be burnt alive. *The Catholic Encyclopedia*

But there's a problem. When you study history books you will find that some maintain that the Roman Catholic church burned a "mere" few hundred people at the stake for what they thought was heresy, while others say it was in the millions.

It is horrific that even one person was burned to death in the name of Christianity. When the disciples asked Jesus if they should call down fire on those who were not of their belief, the Bible says, "But he turned, and rebuked them, and said, 'You know not what manner of spirit you are of. For the Son of man is not come to destroy men's lives, but to save them'" (Luke 9:55-56). When Peter cut off a man's ear with his sword, Jesus healed the man.

Intelligent Life

While talking with fellow entertainers John Belushi, Louis Malle and John Guare, Dan Aykroyd observed that he, Malle and Guare (as well as Adele Guare) had all been raised as Catholics. Some of Dan Aykroyd's family members had been Catholic priests, and he himself was in Catholic Seminary, intending to become a priest, until about the age of seventeen. Aykroyd said they were all "fallen Catholics."[12]

Sadly, there are many fallen Catholics in Hollywood. This is because when religion clashes with someone (as Alan Alda said), it misshapes the head. But sadly it also hardens the heart.

The repulsion of religious institutions is understandable. Religion is number two when it comes to causing wars down through history. Number one is atheistic communism. It

12 Source: Bob Woodward, *Wired: The Short Life and Fast Times of John Belushi*, Simon and Schuster: New York (1984), page 226.

caused more than 100,000,000 deaths. This shows that the problem isn't a political or religious system. It's the human heart.

Man makes a mess of almost everything to which he puts his hand, whether it is politics or religion. I am sure that if we do one day discover intelligent life in the universe, we will start a war with them and kill them. That's the nature of man, and that's why man needs a new nature. But if you are as offended with religion as I am, don't make the mistake of throwing out the baby with the bathwater. There is a wonderful healthy baby of reality and truth in this great ocean of dirty bathwater of hypocrisy and lies.

The Missing Link to Understanding Truth

I was speaking on the subject of intelligent design, standing next to an animated gorilla we called "Link." Suddenly a man appeared in front of him, grabbed both of his arms and dislocated his huge shoulder. I angrily said, "What are you doing? You have dislocated his shoulder!" The man looked confused. Suddenly an older woman appeared with an embarrassed expression on her face, grabbed his hand and said, "I'm so sorry. He's autistic."

Instantly my anger was replaced with empathy, both for the mother and the son. My opinion of him changed because knowledge gave me a different perspective, and that changed my mind in reference to the man.

Knowledge can do that. Are you angered by religious hypocrisy? In a sense you should be. But here's some knowledge that may change your perspective.

Hypocrites are actors. They aren't the genuine article. Think what an actor does. He plays a part. Hypocrites are pretenders playing the part of a Christian, and God warns that the hypocrite will be well-paid for his acting, on Judgment Day. Not one will go to Heaven.

So if you are bothered by religious hypocrisy, know that God is offended by them infinitely more than you are. And take a moment to look at what Scripture says about those who are offended by hypocrites, if there is any hypocrisy in their lives:

> "Therefore you are inexcusable, O man, whosoever you are that judge: for wherein you judge another, you condemn yourself; for you that judge do the same things. But we are sure that the judgment of God is according to truth against them which commit such things. And think this, O man, that judge them which do such things, and do the same, that you shall escape the judgment of God?" (Romans 2:1-3)

Notice now how the Scripture turns the mirror on those that judge the hypocrite:

> "You therefore which teach another, do you not teach yourself? You that preach a man should not steal, do you steal? You that say a man should not commit adultery, do you commit adultery?" (Romans 2:21-22).

Maybe you think that you have the right to judge a hypocrite because you haven't committed adultery. But look at the words of Jesus:

> "You have heard that it was said by them of old time, You shall not commit adultery: But I say to you, That whosoever looks on a woman to lust after her has committed adultery with her already in his heart" (Matthew 5:27-28).

None of us can point a finger at another. None of us can cast the first stone, because none of us is without sin.

So what should be our attitude towards the hypocrite? We should be fearful for him, because he is self-deceiving. What he does and what comes out of his mouth don't match—but this doesn't bother him. Listen to Bono[13] as he shares his thoughts about God and his spirituality:

13　Paul David Hewson KBE (born May 10, 1960), known as Bono, is the lead singer and principal lyricist of the Irish rock band U2. Bono is also widely known for his work as an activist in Africa.

"I'd be in big trouble if Karma was going to finally be my judge. I'd be in deep [expletive]. It doesn't excuse my mistakes, but I'm holding out for Grace. I'm holding out that Jesus took my sins onto the Cross, because I know who I am, and I hope I don't have to depend on my own religiosity.

"But I love the idea of the Sacrificial Lamb. I love the idea that God says: *Look, you cretins, there are certain results to the way we are, to selfishness, and there's a mortality as part of your very sinful nature, and, let's face it, you're not living a very good life, are you? There are consequences to actions.* The point of the death of Christ is that Christ took on the sins of the world, so that what we put out did not come back to us, and that our sinful nature does not reap the obvious death. That's the point. It should keep us humbled … It's not our own good works that get us through the gates of heaven.

"When I look at the Cross of Christ, what I see up there is all my [expletive] and everybody else's. So I ask myself a question a lot of people have asked: Who is this man? And was He who He said He was, or was He just a religious nut? And there it is, and that's the question. And no one can talk you into it or out of it.[14]

> "When I look at the Cross of Christ, what I see up there is all my [expletive] and everybody else's."
> –*Bono*

Again, none of us can point a condemnatory finger of judgment at another who professes to be a Christian. The context of the "judge not lest you be judged," passage of Scripture is in respect to seeing a speck in your Christian brother's eye and trying to get it out when there is a log in your own eye. Jesus said to take the log out first, then you will see clearly and be able to help your bother out.

---

14 *Bono: In Conversation with Michka Assayas* (Riverhead Books, 2006).

However, one should question a person's salvation if he professes to be a Christian but has a filthy mouth. Jesus said that the mouth speaks the abundance of the heart, and a dirty mouth is evidence of a dirty heart.

If someone puts on a parachute and doesn't bother to tighten the straps, it's love and a very real concern that says, "Hey buddy, those straps should be tight!" Anyone who can stand at 10,000 feet on the edge of a plane without his parachute put on properly is either insane or he is ignorant as to the terrible consequences of violating the law of gravity.

Clearly, Bono isn't insane. He is a brilliant musician and a very compassionate human being. His problem is more than likely no one has ever confronted him with the Law of God to show him that the God he so loosely talks about is holy and is to be feared.

Who's in Control?

Those who are concerned that the hypocrite will get what's coming to him can be consoled. The hypocrite will end up in Hell.

When asked for his "notions of heaven and hell, eternal damnation vs. eternal bliss" Keanu Reeves[15] said:

> "Well, I hope I get the bliss. And I know I'm going to have to work for it. But I've got to say, really, I have no kind of, can I say 'secular religiosity'? ... I don't have a denominational sight. I think, like in the stories that we tell, there is an aspect of the living life informing where we go. A transfiguration, there must be. Energy can't be created or destroyed, and energy flows. It must be in a direction, with some kind of internal, emotive, spiritual direction. It must have some effect somewhere. ... I do think there must be some kind of interaction between your living life and the life that goes on from here."

---

15 Keanu Charles Reeves played Neo in the action film trilogy *The Matrix*, Kevin Lomax in *The Devil's Advocate*, and starring roles in *Speed*, *Constantine* and *Bill & Ted's Excellent Adventure*.

When asked for his belief about "the concept of a personal Hell for all eternity" Reeves replied, "No, no, this is not hell. I guess living without love, without experiencing it or being able to give it. I think the aspect of that would be, that's pretty strong punishment."[16]

Hell isn't simply "living without love." If it was, I wouldn't have devoted the last 35 years of my life pleading with people to get right with God. It is a place of eternal torment. Those who are angered by someone who warns about Hell should stop for one moment and ask the question, "What if Hell really does exist? What if God and His Law are holy and perfect?" It would be good for them to consult their own God-given "reason" for a moment. It's the ability to morally reason that separates us from the animals. Think, is it reasonable that if God is good, He must punish murderers who have never been brought to justice? He must also do the same with rapists. He *must* see that justice is done. Even sinful man strives for that. But God's justice won't stop at murderers and rapists. It will also include thieves and liars.

The Dalai Lama

Reincarnation is a popular belief among many celebrities, probably because it deals with the problem of man's sin in a way that excludes any mention of the existence of a horrible place called Hell.

After Barbara Walters hosted a program on the subject of Heaven, she said of the Dalai Lama,

> "I loved his own warm-heartedness, I loved my hand in his, his humor. I sat in the rain with hundreds of Buddhist monks of all ages listening to him. He is very appealing. He says he is not a god, that he is a teacher. He's very modest. If I believed in anything I would believe in reincarnation.

---

16 http://www.beliefnet.com/story/161/story_16124_1.html

That would help explain some of the misery in life ... and that perhaps the next life will be better."[17]

While reincarnation may be appealing and answer some questions, it brings up some more issues—such as who is in charge of giving out all these new bodies? If an evil man comes back as a cockroach, who then is the person or persons in charge of making the moral judgment as to whether or not the man lived a good or evil life. What standard do they judge by? Is it the Ten Commandments? If it's not, then what is the moral standard?

While reincarnation may be appealing to some, it has no grounds in the Word of God, which clearly says that it is appointed to man once to die, and after this comes the judgment.

---

17 http://newsweek.washingtonpost.com/onfaith/guestvoices/2006/12/television_personality_looks_a.html

Can You Name One?

Jay Leno, host of "The Tonight Show," once conducted a man-on-the-street type interview in which he asked young people questions about the Bible. "Can you name one of the Ten Commandments?" he asked two college-age women. One replied, "Freedom of speech?" Mr. Leno said to the other, "Complete this sentence: Let him who is without sin..." Her response was, "have a good time?" Jay Leno then turned to a young man and asked, "Who, according to the Bible, was eaten by a whale?" The confident answer was, "Pinocchio."

Our problem in America is that we have what the Bible calls a "form of godliness." We have preachers in pulpits who have become nothing more than effective motivational speakers. They will tell you how to find success in money matters and marriage, but they rarely speak of the subjects they have been entrusted with—the Ten Commandments, Judgment Day, the cross, or the necessity of repentance and faith to find everlasting life, and this has had its effect on society.

Look at Winona Rider's answer when it comes to the subject of faith in God, as she was interviewed by "Entertainment Tonight":

> **Winona:** "Well, it seems like everyone ends up rebelling against it when they're raised so strictly with it. You know, Madonna, perfect example … she's done everything from embracing it to rebelling to shocking. But I appreciate all

> "I appreciate all different religions and I think you should take what you can from each one of them and make up your own."
> –Winona Rider

different religions and I think you should take what you can from each one of them and make up your own."

ET: "A la carte. So this movie's a lot about faith. Talk to me about faith … Do you have faith? Faith in what?"

Winona: "That's a very difficult question, because faith is so associated with religion. When you hear the word, you automatically think of … But I think of it as believing in something, and I certainly have that. I have faith in myself, my family, my friends—it's kind of a boring answer, but it's too difficult."[1]

When Tom Cruise was asked about his faith and whether or not his Scientology was a religion, he said:

> "It is not a matter of, 'There is no God.' There is a God, okay?"
> –Tom Cruise

"It is a religion. It is not a matter of, 'There is no God.' There is a God, okay? But there are things where there are … that is why I say you have to read what Scientology is, because it is non-denominational. There are Jewish Scientologists. There are Christian Scientologists. There are Baptist Scientologists.

"What it comes down to is, 'What do you know?' I don't care about what other people say. I don't live my life based on what other people think I should do, okay? I live my life based on what I know is right for myself. And what I care about is other people. And I care about my family and I care about the world and I want to see it a better place. And

---

1 http://browsers.netscape.com/etonline/interviews/winonaryder/
winonaryder_int5.html

I don't care what people say. I know what Scientology is. It is extraordinary, what it has done."[2]

The tragedy with ignorance about God is that one can find extraordinary success in life, but when the big storms hit, "success" means nothing.

One of Hollywood's most fun-loving, successful and talented stars was Fred Astaire. Although he was rich and famous, life's biggest tragedy hit him like a freight train between the eyes. He was married and it was said of his wife, "Phyllis was just what Fred needed. She became his buffer against the unpleasant things of the world. Fred worshiped and respected her. He phoned her from the studio every day at lunchtime." But one day death snatched her from his hands.

> In New York, [Fred Astaire] often sat for hours in the quiet of St. Bartholomew's Episcopal Church on Park Avenue. He explained to interviewer Bill Davidson: "I find great comfort in that magnificent church in the midst of the hurly-burly of the city. I think of everything there—my life, my work, the hidden meaning of the good and bad things that have happened to me. I come out spiritually refreshed. It often helps me to go on." In Beverly Hills, he spent long hours of contemplation in his parish church, All Saints, on Santa Monica Boulevard.
>
> About eleven o'clock the next morning, as Engel was gloomily sitting in his office, Fred walked in. "I don't know if I can make it, Sam, but I'll try. I'm reporting for work."
>
> Engel said: It was a frightful ordeal for the poor man. He'd be dancing as if nothing had happened, and then he'd come over in a corner and talk to me. He'd say, "I don't know if Old Dad can make it," and tears would come to his eyes. I'd say, "It's okay. It's all right to cry." He'd say, "It's rough, Sam, real rough. Especially going home and she's not there." Then he'd talk about how Phyllis wanted him to make this picture, and he'd go back to work. When

---

Daddy Long Legs was finally released, Fred was so good in it that I'm sure the audience never guessed his heart was breaking. His class emerged when he wrote me a letter saying, "Thanks for standing by Old Dad." It should have been the other way around.

Randolph Scott remembered those days: "After Daddy Long Legs was finished, Fred used to go to the cemetery and sit at Phyllis's grave for hours at a time."

After much research I came up with no references to Fred Astaire's personal faith in God, although it's clear that he wasn't an atheist. He did hope that God would heal his wife when she was deathly sick, but when that didn't happen, he was understandably devastated.

The Power of Faith

Faith in God is a buffer against life's biggest storms. It's far more than mustering up an intellectual "belief" in a God we cannot see. Think of a man who has no faith in an elevator. He doesn't trust the cables. He is convinced that they will snap. That man will be fearful to step into the elevator. Now think of a man who knows the cables are trustworthy. He has spoken to the maker and has seen that each of the 26 cables is made of inch thick steal. Just one cable has the strength to support more than twenty tons, let alone the half a ton that a full elevator weighs ... and there are 26 cables, with a high-tech automatic breaking system that will kick in the moment something even goes slightly wrong. That man has no fear as long as he has faith. The more faith, the less fear.

If you have a living faith in the risen Jesus Christ, then death won't devastate you when it comes to you or to those you love. But more than that: If those you love also have faith in Jesus, you will be unspeakably comforted in their death. You will have (beyond the shadow of a doubt) a wonderful hope in Christ that you will see them again, and it won't be as a ghost in some nebulous place called "Heaven." Heaven is "down to earth." God's Kingdom is coming to this earth. God's will *will be done* on this earth, as it is in Heaven. New bodies are promised to all who love the Savior—bodies that will not age or be subject to disease and death. Hard to believe? But it is the gospel truth.

Look what the Bible says to those who have this hope in Christ, calling death simply a "sleep":

> But I would not have you to be ignorant, brethren, concerning them which are asleep, that you sorrow not, even as others which have no hope. For if we believe that Jesus died and rose again, even so them also which sleep in Jesus will God bring with him. For this we say unto you by the word of the Lord, that we which are alive and remain unto the coming of the Lord shall not prevent them which are asleep. For the Lord himself shall descend from heaven with a shout, with the voice of the archangel, and with the trump of God: and the dead in Christ shall rise first: Then we which are alive and remain shall be caught up together with them in the clouds, to meet the Lord in the air: and so shall we ever be with the Lord. Wherefore comfort one another with these words (1 Thessalonians 4:13-18).

Julie Andrews was another celebrity who was tragically left in the darkness when it came to the things of God. Her first marriage took place in an Anglican church, but there is little indication that she was even nominally Anglican.

She had no religious upbringing whatsoever (her only prayers were just before going on stage: "Oh, God, don't let me fall on my face"). But she did become a zealous convert to psychoanalysis. "I'm only beginning to crystallize the bits and pieces of my life," she said, "and analysis helps. I think I'd have been a rotten mother without analysis. I do have phobias, and there's no doubt about it. I have enormous phobias about singing, stemming from the Broadway days when I was trotted out every night and was pretty much mixed up."

After twelve years of her second marriage and her expanded family life, Julie's priorities were clear at last. While she would undoubtedly continue to make forays into the show-business world that had been with her literally her whole life, she said, "I certainly wouldn't compare the rewards of watching one's children grow up and mature with that of money piling up at the box office. Both are pleasant, but to varying degrees.

"As the old saying goes, you can't take the audience home with you. You can't depend on the loyalty of fans, who, after all is said and done, are just faceless people one seldom sees. And few stars have their fans forever. But a child is forever; that bond and relationship is timeless and doesn't depend on your looks, age or popularity at the moment."[3]

The problem is that the bond with our loved ones isn't "forever." Forever is a word that can only be rightly used by those who are in a right relationship with God. Everything else that this Godless world clings to is temporal.

The Waiter

It is normal for secular humanity to use God as a celestial Waiter. This can only end in disillusionment. Look at these tragic and telling words from screen legend Greta Garbo:

"...God? Who is He? What roads does He travel? Why do we talk all the time about Someone whom no one has ever seen? True, I have heard Him many times, but I have never seen Him. Now, as I advance in age, His voice is becoming clearer. Yet I cannot allow myself to follow His voice, for if I do, I will not be myself. I would like to meet Him face to face, because I would have many questions to ask Him. Questions only He can answer, burning questions for me. He is supposed to be wise and just in everything. But why has He given to people the idea that the artist is

---

3 Robert Windeler, *Julie Andrews: A Biography*, St. Martin's Press: New York (1983).

inspired by God and that artists are cousins of God who try to make interpretations of His beauty? Why is the artist, more than other people, tortured by life? Is this the doing of a just God?

"Why did God create in me the desire to act? And why in film? Why did a wise God push me into the hands of Mauritz Stiller, who, as I look back, was most likely an instrument of Satan? I can remember what Stiller said to me: 'For us film is a miracle created by Satan—the greatest miracle, which can capture human emotions and happiness faithfully, more faithfully than any other medium. And I am sure film is more suited for the art of depravity than for the art of godly justice.'

> "Why did God create in me the desire to act?"
> –Greta Garbo

"I am so confused now, because, though he was anti-God, it was through Moje [Stiller] that I became famous. Then he left me without reaping any reward for his work on my talent and on my spiritual and physical appearance. I was abandoned in this world like a corps of leaderless soldiers, like a tiger without a head. Yet other thoughts tell me that I don't need a leader anymore, that I don't even need a head.

"I have lost a belief in people, in a God who put me in this situation without replying clearly to my questions. I am floating on the waters of life without direction, without a goal, without the knowledge of why and how long.[4]

---

4 Mauritz Stiller (July 17, 1883–November 18, 1928) was an actor, screenwriter and an influential silent film director. Born Moshe Stiller in Helsinki, Finland, he was the son of Russian-Polish Jewish parents. At age four, his mother committed suicide and he was raised by family friends. Drafted into the Russian army of Czar Nicholas II, rather than report for duty he fled the country and settled in Sweden. By 1912 Stiller had become involved with Sweden's rapidly developing silent film industry. He began by writing scripts, plus acting and directing in short films, but within a few years gave up on acting to devote his time to writing and directing. He was soon directing feature-length productions and his 1918 effort *Thomas Graals bästa barn* (*Thomas Graal's First Child*) with Victor Sjöström in the leading role, received much acclaim. By 1920, having directed more than thirty-five films, Stiller was a leading figure in Swedish filmmaking. At the Royal Dramatic Theatre in Stockholm he met a young actress named Greta

Garbo was one of Hollywood's first (and biggest) of its carefully crafted golden calves. But once again, her image was unreal. Despite her incredible success, she ended up totally disillusioned with life. Sylvester Stallone said, "When you make it big in Hollywood, it's like you have keys to the candy store. Your morals get corrupted, and you start believing your own hype. You surround yourself with people who will tell you what you want to hear. Hollywood is isolated and money-driven, and faith is certainly not up at the forefront.[5]

Greta Garbo's statement "True, I have heard Him many times, but I have never seen Him" reveals a shallow understanding of the Biblical revelation of God. The Bible says that we cannot see God and live. This is because of our sinfulness.

Think of a devious criminal that has raped, murdered and then decapitated five teenage girls. The man is not insane. He said he loved what he did, and he would do it again if he had half a chance.

Think now of the most righteous and good judge who is presiding over his case. At his summation, he looks at the weeping parents and families of the innocent victims he so viciously brutalized. He looks at pictures of their mutilated bodies. He studies the fingerprint evidence on the knife he used to cut the throats of his terrified victims.

He then turns his attention to the smiling murderer. How is he going to feel towards this man? If he has an ounce of goodness he is going to be wrath-filled. The depth of his anger will be in direct proportion to his goodness.

Gustafsson whom he cast in an important but secondary role in his film, *Gösta Berlings saga (The Atonement of Gosta Berling)* giving her the stage name Greta Garbo. For Stiller, the screen presence of the eighteen-year-old actress led to him bringing her to the United States after he accepted an offer from studio boss Louis B. Mayer to direct for MGM. http://en.wikipedia.org/wiki/Mauritz_Stiller

5 http://www.christianlivingmag.com

That's why sinful men and women can't stand before a holy God. The fire of His righteous indignation (His absolute goodness) would spill over on us because of our sin.

When Moses asked to see God, He was told that he couldn't see Him and live.[6] Then God put Moses in the cleft of a rock, and let His "goodness" pass by, and Moses was then allowed to look at where God's goodness had been. As he came down from the mountain after that experience, Israel couldn't look at the face of Moses because it so glowed, because he had merely gazed at where God had been. Jesus said, "Blessed are the pure in heart, for they shall see God." The only way sinful men and women can stand before God and not be consumed by the fire of His holy wrath is to be pure of heart. How can that happen? That's another issue we will look at later on in this book.

---

6 "And [Moses] said, I beseech you, show me your glory. And he said, I will make all my goodness pass before you, and I will proclaim the name of the LORD before you; and will be gracious to whom I will be gracious, and will show mercy on whom I will show mercy. And he said, You can not see my face: for there shall no man see me, and live" (Exodus 33:18-20).

The Ten Commandments

Cecil B. DeMille was called "the greatest director of them all." As he was preparing his studio to film *The Ten Commandments*[1] he sent a copy of the Bible to every single person on the payroll, with the words, "As I intend to film practically the entire book of Exodus…the Bible should never be away from you. Place it on your desk, and when you travel, stick in your briefcase. Make reading it a daily habit."[2]

Director John Huston received fifteen Oscar nominations in the course of his career. In looking at his movies, one could easily have thought that he had some sort of faith in God. He directed *Let There Be Light* (1946), *Beat the Devil* (1953), *Heaven Knows, Mr. Allison* (1957), *The Roots of Heaven* (1958), *The Unforgiven* (1960), *The Bible: In The Beginning* (1966), *Sinful Davey* (1969).

He also directed *The Misfits,* which had an all-star cast including Clark Gable, Marilyn Monroe, Montgomery Clift, and Eli Wallach. It was said that Huston spent long evenings carousing in the Nevada casinos after filming, surrounded by reporters and beautiful women, gambling, drinking, and smoking cigars. Gable remarked during this time that "if he

---

1 DeMille once said, "Give me any two pages of the Bible, and I'll give you a picture." http://www.csmonitor.com/2006/1013/p11s01-almo.html

2 Charles Higham, *Cecil B. DeMille: A Biography of the Most Successful Film Maker of Them All,* Charles Scribner's Sons: New York (1973), pages 111-114.

kept it up he would soon die of it." Ironically, and tragically, Gable died three weeks after the end of filming from a massive heart attack, while Huston went on to live for twenty-six more years.[3]

Huston's irreverence [while filming and discussing his movie *The Bible*] led to questions about his own faith. On several occasions, he was disarmingly forthright. "Every day I'm being asked if I am a believer and I answer I have nothing in common with Cecil B. DeMille. Actually, I find it foolishly impudent to speculate on the existence of any kind of God..."[4]

It *is* foolish to speculate on the existence of any kind of God. His existence is axiomatic. Huston was right, although he no doubt was speaking from the point of view of atheism. DeMille was no atheist:

Unlike the first Exodus [in DeMille's 1923 version of *The Ten Commandments*], the new one went off without a hitch. Then, one day, DeMille had a horrifying experience. In order to check a faulty camera, he climbed with Henry Wilcoxon to the very top of one of the one-hundred-three-foot gates, up an almost perpendicular ladder—an extraordinary feat for a man of his years. As he reached the top and looked down through the brilliant sunlight on the immense multitude he felt an almost overwhelming sense of pride. But a terrible pain suddenly shot through the very center of his heart. He staggered, and his face turned green. He began to bend over; the pain was more intense than anything he had felt in his life. For a moment, he was unable to breathe ... Mustering his extraordinary will power, praying deeply and from the

---

3   He died from emphysema on August 28, 1987 in Middletown, Rhode Island, at the age of 81. His body is interred in the Hollywood Forever Cemetery in Hollywood, California.

4   Axel Madsen, *John Huston: A Biography*, Doubleday and Company: Garden City, New York (1978), page 212.

essence of his being to God, he made the descent, then sank miserably to a sitting position.

That night, DeMille went into his bedroom and prayed as he had never prayed before in his life. We will never know what he asked God to provide, but it may be imagined that he called upon all the strength that lay within his being, that he sought to draw up power from the very wellsprings of life itself. As dawn broke—the acrid, flatly-lit dawn of Egypt—he stood up in his room and cried out. When he took Cecilia's hands in his own later that morning, he knew that he had been spared: his will, just as it had triumphed over rheumatic fever and exhaustion in 1921, had triumphed again.

God spared him and he was able to finish the movie. Some time later, as he lay on his deathbed, he was alone with a nurse:

> He began to scribble some notes on a piece of paper. They read: "The Lord giveth and the Lord taketh away. Blessed be the name of the Lord. It can only be a short time…until those words, the first in the Episcopal funeral services are spoken over me…. After those words are spoken, what am I? I am only what I have accomplished. How much good have I spread? How much evil have I spread? For whatever I am a moment after death—a spirit, a soul, a bodiless mind—I shall have to look back and forward, for I have to take with me both."[5]

The Ten Commandments was a powerful portrayal of the life of Moses. However, the film was aptly titled because Moses was merely the deliverer of a divine message. We should therefore honor him as the delivery man, and then look closely at the gift God gave through him.

Ask most people for their thoughts on the purpose of the Ten Commandments, and they will tell you that they were

---

5 Higham, page 307.

given as a moral code by which we should strive to live. Listen to Humphrey Bogart's son talk of the basis for his father's ethics:

> "My father was also a 'personal-religionist,' which is a phrase I never heard until I read it in a press release about him. Basically, it means he didn't practice his religion … 'Bogie was not a religious man,' my mother says. 'But he was a great believer in the Ten Commandments and the Golden Rule.'"
>
> Nat Benchley says, "His moral code was strict, and was based on, and almost indistinguishable from, the Ten Commandments. He didn't always obey them, but he believed in them."[6]

> "Bogie was not a religious man," my mother says. "But he was a great believer in the Ten Commandments and the Golden Rule."
> –Stephen Humphrey Bogart

Who of us isn't a believer in the Ten Commandments? As moral beings, we can't find fault with Thou shalt not steal, Thou shalt not lie, etc. No sane person can claim ignorance of God's Law because it's written on our hearts.[7] While many may deny the existence of Heaven and Hell, few deny the reality of their personal conscience. This is never more evident than when a secular person talks about their own moral virtues. Bette Davis' father was an atheist, but she didn't follow in his steps:

> In 1985, following her stroke, a reporter asked Bette if she was religious. She acknowledged that she was, but not in the traditional sense. She wasn't much of a churchgoer, and she did not believe in life after death or in Heaven and Hell. "All

---

6 *Bogart: In Search of My Father* by Stephen Humphrey Bogart and Gary Provost. New York, NY: Dutton, 1995. Pages 152-153.

7 See Romans 2:15

my life," she said, "morality has been more important to me than religion; honesty, integrity, character—old-fashioned virtues preached by people like Emerson, Thoreau, and my New England grandmother."

When asked, months before her death, if she believed in God, Bette replied, "Oh, of course! Of course! My religious beliefs can be capsulized in two ways. One is 'To thine own self be true' and 'God helps those who help themselves.'

> When asked...if she believed in God, Bette [Davis] replied, "Oh, of course! Of course!"

Another is 'You get back what you give'—not always true."[8]

True to Whom?

The popular saying "To thine own self be true"[9] sounds virtuous, but it is very subjective. Was Hitler true to himself? Did he live by what he believed? Where does the conscience come into play with such a life-philosophy? What if a man's conscience does allow him to do things that are reprehensible? The Bible speaks of an "evil" conscience (trying to cover sin by good works) and a conscience that has been "seared" (lost its outward life). We can dull the voice of the conscience.

So the only reliable guide to what is right and what is wrong is the Ten Commandments. The fact that they were written in stone speaks of their immutability. It was by those Commandments that I personally saw that I needed God's forgiveness. Without them, I was convinced that I was being true to myself.

---

8 Randall Riese, *All About Bette: Her Life from A to Z*, Contemporary Books: Chicago (1993), pages 370-371.

9 When prompting people to follow their conscience on matters, the oft-touted "To thine own self be true" is occasionally cited as a Biblical recommendation, but it is not from the Bible. In truth, this saying originates in the Shakespearean tragedy *Hamlet*. Polonius, the older counselor of Prince Hamlet's uncle, King Claudius, is in the midst of dispensing advice to the prince when he speaks forth the famous line: "This above all things: to thine own self be true" (*Hamlet*, 3.1.81).

As we have seen, the reason that each of us needs God's forgiveness is because the Bible warns that He is good and will therefore one day see that justice is done—He will punish murderers, rapists, thieves and liars. So, how will you do on that day? This is the most important question you will ever be asked, because your innocence or your guilt will determine your eternal destiny. So it's in your very best interests to look into the question with an honest heart. You can find how you will do simply by looking at the Ten Commandments and using them as a mirror to see yourself in truth.

Hopefully, every morning you take the time to look into a mirror so that you will be respectable in the sight of man, so look for a moment into the mirror of the Ten Commandments to see if you are respectable in the sight of God. If your mirror reveals dirt, it sends you to the water to wash. Do the same with God's Moral Law. Let it show you if you need cleansing. So here goes. We are going to turn the mirror towards you. It may not be a pleasant sight, but look into it, and let it send you to the Savior for cleansing.

Have you loved God above all else? Is He first in your life? Do you love Him with all of your heart, mind, soul and strength? Or have you made a god in your mind that you're comfortable with, a god to suit yourself? Jesus said, "Whoever looks upon a woman to lust after her has committed adultery with her already in his heart"[10] (the Seventh Commandment includes sex before marriage). Have you ever looked with lust at someone? Have you ever stolen anything? Have you lied (including answering these questions)? Have you always honored your parents, and kept the Sabbath holy? Have you coveted other people's things? Have you ever used God's holy name in vain, using it as a cuss word to express disgust? If you have, think of what you have done. He gave you life itself and every pleasure you have ever had, and you equated

---

10 Matthew 5:27, 28.

His name with a four-lettered filth word, something called "blasphemy."

Here now is the big question. On Judgment Day, will you be found to be innocent or guilty? Think for a moment before you answer. Will you end up in Heaven or Hell? If you somehow think that all will be well, please realize that it will not. The Bible warns that all liars, thieves, and adulterers will end up in Hell.[11] Can you see the dirt? Do you see that you need to be cleansed?

Here is the "water" that God provided for your cleansing. The Bible says that God Himself made a way where His justice and His mercy could meet. We broke the Law, but He became a man to pay the fine in His life's blood. Jesus suffered and died on the cross to satisfy the Moral Law—"For God so loved the world that He gave His only begotten Son, that whosoever believes in Him should not perish but have everlasting life."[12] Then He rose from the dead, defeating death. That means that God can forgive you and grant you the gift of everlasting life.[13] He can "justify" you, cleanse you, and give you the "righteousness" of Christ. That means you can have more than your sins *forgiven*. God can make it as though you *never* sinned in the first place by giving you the righteousness of His Son. *He can make you pure of heart, so that you can stand in His holy presence.*

What we must do is repent of our sins (turn from them), and receive the gift of eternal life by trusting the person of Jesus Christ alone. That means you forsake your own good works as a means of trying to please God, and trust in the Savior only. You are a guilty criminal before a holy God, therefore any good works you offer the Judge are detestable acts of bribery. Don't offer them. Simply throw yourself on His mercy, and the Bible says that He's rich in mercy to all who call upon

---

11 Revelation 21:8, 1 Corinthians 6:9-10

12 John 3:16

13 Ephesians 2:8-9, Romans 6:23

Him. So *call* upon Him now. Please, confess your sins to God right now, put your trust in Jesus to save you, and you will pass from death to life. Then read the Bible daily and obey what you read.[14] Pray something like this: "Dear God, today I turn away from all of my sins (name them) and I put my trust in Jesus Christ as my Lord and Savior. Please forgive me, change my heart, and grant me Your gift of everlasting life. In Jesus' name I pray. Amen."

---

14   See John 14:21

A sk anyone who finds themselves in the contemporary movie industry and they will tell you that they have temptations that the average person doesn't have to deal with. Hollywood *leads* its actors into temptation. It *delivers* them to evil. If they had a spark of faith when they arrived in the dark town, it is soon put out by pressure to conform and by the extracurricular celebrity lifestyle.

Before *Everybody Loves Raymond* made her a star, Patricia Heaton (raised Catholic, now a practicing Presbyterian) was sent a film script that she felt was exploitative. Though broke, she never auditioned, and after persisting she eventually found a home on *Raymond*—one of the few shows to depict churchgoing as a matter of course. "Most people have some kind of faith," she says. "It makes the show more real." Keeping the faith in Hollywood, though, poses special challenges. "This business tests you constantly: the materialism, the pride, the ambition," says Heaton.[1]

Clint Eastwood had a family background that was sprinkled with devout believers, but for some reason there doesn't seem to be much faith in his personal background.

When David Frost mulled over the subject of God with him in one of his prestigious television interviews, Clint began to mumble and fall back on nature as his main spiritual source.

---

1 http://www.mastermediaintl.org/guest/MLPC/PeopleMag.html

When Frost asked if religion was important to him, he was uncomfortable:

> "I take it in a personal way very much," said Clint. "I'm just not a member of an organized religion. But I've always felt very strongly about things, I guess. Especially when I'm out in nature. I guess that's why I've done so many wide open films in nature. But religion is, I think, a very personal thing. I've never really discussed it to philosophize out loud about it.
>
> "I just kind of … you're sitting on a beautiful mountain, or in the Rocky Mountains, or wherever, and you…the Grand Canyon is something … and all of a sudden you can't help but be moved. An awful lot of time has gone by on this planet, and mankind's part of it was all about like that [snaps fingers]. And so you think, 'How did that all come to be?' So you can go on forever, within your mind, but it's fun to philosophize on it, as long as you don't, it doesn't drive you to jump off the cliff."[2]

> "But religion is, I think, a very personal thing. I've never really discussed it to philosophize out loud about it."
> –Clint Eastwood

Who doesn't sit in awe and watch a sunrise? Or who doesn't stand in wonder on the edge of the Grand Canyon, or gaze into the heavens at the edge of our universe and not be moved? Conscience demands some sort of acknowledgement to something or Someone somewhere for creation.

Harrison Ford, one of Hollywood's most successful movie actors, found stardom in *Star Wars, Indiana Jones,* and many other films. In a 2002 interview, Ford spoke of finding "the notion of divinity" on his 800-acre ranch in Jackson Wyoming:

---

2 Patrick McGilligan, *Clint: The Life and Legend*, St. Martin's Press: New York (1999), page 29.

"My great interest in the environment came from being in Jackson. I'd purchased land and had a sense of stewardship about the place, because the majesty of nature is so apparent there. It helped sensitize me to the greater needs of the earth. I have a sense of awe, a sense that nature is so complex and fascinating that it's as close as I've come to understanding the notion of divinity."[3]

The Conscience

Each of us has this small voice that tells us when we do something wrong. It acts completely independent of our will. We want to do things we know are wrong, and the conscience stands like an impartial judge on the courtroom of the mind and points an accusing finger. It gives a guilty verdict:

> "I have a sense of awe, a sense that nature is so complex and fascinating that it's as close as I've come to understanding the notion of divinity."
> –Harrison Ford

My conscience hath a thousand several tongues,
And every tongue brings in a several tale,
And every tale condemns me for a villain.
Perjury, perjury, in the high'st degree
Murder, stem murder, in the direst degree;
All several sins, all used in each degree,
Throng to the bar, crying all, Guilty! guilty![4]

Where does *that* fit in the evolutionary philosophy? Why should sane human beings have this voice that tells us not to lie, steal, kill, and not to commit adultery. Where does guilt and morality fit into the cold, cruel ethics-free "survival of the fittest"? Atheists are forced to say that the conscience is socially taught. However, if a child isn't taught this moral code he doesn't live a life free from any form of guilt. He still has an independent conscience.

---

3 http://home.utm.net/pan/pantheistic.html
4 William Shakespeare *King Richard III. Act V, Scene 3.*

Hollywood has deadened its conscience. Jesus said, "But if your eye be evil, your whole body shall be full of darkness. If therefore the light that is in you [the conscience] be darkness, how great is that darkness!"[5]

Divine Connection

Bette Midler knew the power of her conscience (and its divine association), when she transgressed its voice. In high school a friend of hers invited her to go shoplifting at the mall:

> "The thing that's satisfying is your relationship with your God..."
> –Bette Midler

"... But I didn't really like it. It was too terrifying. It hurt my nerves. I stopped and I've never stolen anything since. I would never, ever think of it. After my girlfriend and I took this makeup—lipsticks and hair dye—from the mall, we were on our way home with our little bags. It was pouring rain, we were in the middle of a hurricane, and my girlfriend and I got down on our knees and said, 'God, if you don't kill us in this hurricane we swear we will never do this again.' We didn't die and we never did it again. I keep my vows.

"The thing that's satisfying is your relationship with your God, your planet, your family, your friends and how you see beauty and how you see the world. You come down from that perch a little and give that up. You can't eat your newspaper clippings. And you can't take your newspaper clippings to bed. It's really not that satisfying."[6]

Eddie, Johnny, Jane, and Prayer

Not only do we all have a conscience, but each of us has an instinct that we have come from some sort of greater Being. Statistics tell us that almost everybody prays. Most pray daily. They pray for themselves, for their family, for material things,

---

5 Matthew 6:23

6 George Mair, *Bette: An Intimate Biography of Bette Midler*, Birch Lane Press/Carol Publishing Group: Secaucus, NJ (1995).

and for protection, and they pray believing that God hears their prayers. But contrary to common (and popular) belief, the Bible says that God deliberately rejects the prayers of those who continue in sin.[7]

When Johnny Depp[8] was asked if he had faith in God, he answered:

> "Nothing with a name. I haven't found that, but I hope there's something else out there. I hope that when we leave this world we go on a little trip. Why not? Countless people have had near death experiences and have come back to say they saw interesting things. Nobody returns from the dead and says, 'Hey, there's nothing else.' And while there's no organized religion I agree with, I think the Bible is a very good book. Probably a novel.

> "I pray on airplanes. I get instant religion during takeoff, then when we're safely in the air I sit there thinking about the fact that any little thing that goes wrong could send us crashing to the ground."[9]

> "...while there's no organized religion I agree with, I think the Bible is a very good book."
> –Johnny Depp

Jane Fonda prayed regularly:

> "Well, a lot of times it's thanks. You know, I feel uncomfortable always asking for something [laughs] ... But when I need an answer, or I need someone to be helped,

---

7 See Psalm 66:18

8 Johnny Depp's critical acclaim as an actor garnered him a slew of nominations and awards. He was honored with the 1990 ShoWest Male Star of Tomorrow award, the 1996 London Critics Circle Actor of the Year award for *Ed Wood*, and the 1998 Honorary Cesar. He was nominated for an unprecedented seven Golden Globes, including four consecutive nominations between 2003 and 2006, and two Oscars for his performances in *Pirates of the Caribbean: The Curse of the Black Pearl* (2003) and *Finding Neverland* (2004).

9 http://www.angelfire.com/film/depfan/playboy2.htm

it's always the same: my hands in prayer position and my thumbs pressed against my third eye, my forehead. I find that I need to do that. And I need to be sitting or kneeling. It's like sending up. It's like my prayer and my thoughts go from my head through my fingers upward. And I'm sending this upward and as I describe within the book, I feel 'hooked up.'"[10]

Eddie Murphy admits that he prays. So do his parents, but they were horrified when they first heard the content of their famous son's comedy act. They tried to justify the filth by saying that he didn't use dirty language around the home. His mother said, "Eddie is a firm believer in God and prayer. That's probably why he's so hot today."

She was right about his beliefs:

> "I'm not a religious fanatic, but I pray. I pray every night. And I respect the Church."
> –Eddie Murphy

For all the raunch in his standup routine, offstage Murphy is apparently deeply religious. One Christmas, during a heart-to-heart with Vernon Jr., his brother dismissed the value of prayer. Eddie was shocked and said, "You mean you don't pray every night? I do."

Murphy was profane, but he wasn't blasphemous—a seemingly semantic difference, but not really. Just as he was shocked when his brother told him he didn't pray every night, Murphy showed a respect for religion on and offstage that was reverential, bordering on the superstitious. As he drove past St. Patrick's cathedral in New York with a reporter, he suddenly pushed the eject button on his cassette deck which was playing a raunchy song by Prince. The lyrics were about to launch into a string of expletives, and Murphy explained, "It's a lot

---

10 http://www.beliefnet.com/story/165/story_16529_2.html

of profanity getting ready to come onto the stereo. Can't play it in front of a church.[11]

"I'm not a religious fanatic, but I pray. I pray every night. And I respect the Church. I won't have Prince singing, 'I want to f--- you' in front of it.'"

Balancing the Scales

Most people think that God hears their prayers, and that he simply requires them to live a good life. My pre-Christian philosophy was that if someone believed in God and tried to live a good life, they would go to Heaven ... if there was one.

Probably the most misunderstood issue when it comes to the subject of God and of going to Heaven is that of "living a good life"—or what the Bible refers to as "self-righteousness."

Most secular and religious people (as apposed to Christian people), have the belief that to get to Heaven or to please God, we have to be "good." However, good works (good things we do) have nothing to do with anyone's salvation.[12]

Many actors become pious in their old age. It's human nature to think that if I have lived a sinful lifestyle when I was young, it makes sense that I need to balance the scales when I grow older by doing good things for others. Good works will always be commended by the world, but they can *never* commend us to God. There's a good reason for this that we will look at soon. Before we do, look at how the good works of Elizabeth Taylor bring instant commendation:

Elizabeth Taylor did appear to be making her most triumphant comeback. She was sober, she was lighter, she was beautiful, and she'd had a spiritual awakening. "I believe in a higher power," Elizabeth said. "I believe in one God. I'm so glad I asked for help." Her willingness to seek help from

---

11 Frank Sanello, *Eddie Murphy: The Life and Times of a Comic on the Edge*, Carol Publishing Group: Secaucus, New Jersey (1997).

12 See Ephesians 2:8-9

> "I believe in one God. I'm so glad I asked for help."
> –Elizabeth Taylor

a power greater than herself would impact the rest of her life, changing her into the kind of person who'd help save others from drugs and alcohol and raise millions of dollars for people suffering from AIDS. AA's big message is that one should give rather than take, understand rather than be understood, and love rather than be loved. Liberating one from unrealistic expectations, the program also liberates one from disappointment. "Finally, give of yourself," Elizabeth wrote. "There are many organizations that need help ... Nothing will raise your self-esteem as much as helping others. It will make you like yourself more and make you more likeable ... BFC [Betty Ford Clinic] changed my life."

By now her good works were so well-known that she seemed immune to scandal. "God must have some reason for keeping me alive," she observed. "Something He wants me to do. And I'll know. I'll know. I just have to be still. God knows where we all are." As she regained her strength she realized, "I've got to do something to help people who are *really* sick ..."[13]

---

13 Ellis Auburn, *The Most Beautiful Woman in the World: The Obsessions, Passions, and Courage of Elizabeth Taylor*, HarperCollins Publishers: New York, NY (2000).

Praying Atheists

There aren't too many open atheists in Hollywood. The few who have come out of the closet are Woody Allen, Marlon Brando, George Carlin, Marlene Dietrich, Jodie Foster, Katherine Hepburn and one or two others. But don't ask atheists how many of them exist in Hollywood, or in the U.S. They tend to exaggerate. Some say there are between twenty and thirty million (they lump in agnostics).

CNN said that studies show that there's more like three million, and I don't even believe there's that many. When I talk to those who profess to be atheists, I find that they doubt their lack of faith and often waver into agnosticism ... and many of them aren't even sure about that.

In February of 2007, ABC's *Nightline* received more than 11,000 emails about an item they aired called "The Blasphemy Challenge." Hundreds of professing atheists had recorded themselves on video saying things like "I blaspheme the Holy Spirit, and I'm not afraid." It was a sad and pathetic sight to see so many who felt so strongly about the subject.

I had contacts at ABC, so I proposed a debate. I told them that actor Kirk Cameron and I would like to fly the two atheists who started the challenge to Los Angeles for a public debate on the existence of God. I then quoted one of them as saying, "If they want to come to the table and present their evidence, I will present my evidence. And we will see how much of theirs is based on faith, and how much of mine is based on fact."

We qualified to "come to the table." Kirk is an ex-atheist. I wrote the book, *God Doesn't Believe in Atheists...proof the atheist doesn't exist*, and I had spoken at Yale University on the subject of atheism. I said:

> "Let's hear their best evidence as to why God doesn't exist, and let the audience decide whose evidence is based on faith and whose is based on fact. We cannot only prove that God exists, but we can prove that the atheist doesn't. That's a simple thing to do. I have seen 'atheists' backslide when I have done it (we have it on film).
>
> "One other thing—they say that Christians 'vilify' them. We certainly won't. We have the utmost respect for atheists, since I was treated so well by American Atheists, Inc., when they flew me from Los Angeles to Orlando, Florida to be a platform speaker at their 2001 National Convention.[1]
>
> "They not only put me in a nice hotel, but they had a fruit basket waiting for me, a welcome card, and they treated me with great kindness. We want to do the same for Brian and Kelly."

ABC loved the idea.

Think for a moment what these atheists had done. Hundreds of them put video clips of themselves on YouTube, boldly giving their names and showing their faces, saying, "I blaspheme the Holy Spirit, and I'm not afraid." This was huge news. It could be far-reaching—even to the Middle East—that hundreds of Americans are blaspheming the name of God (the Holy Spirit *is* God). If it became news in the Middle East it would be streamed in Arabic, and the loose translation on the bottom of the screen would probably be "I blaspheme Allah (Allah is Arabic for 'God'), and I am not afraid."

Of course no one in his right mind would ever be so insensitive as to blaspheme Islam. They know that heads would roll.

---

1 http://www.americanatheist.org/conv27/

The reality is that atheists in America know that when they mock the beliefs of genuine Christians, we are going to love them anyway. They know that we are commanded to love even our enemies, and do good to those that despitefully use us. When they strike us on the cheek, we are going to turn the other cheek. And so they have free course to mock that which is dear to us.

But we do take the subject very seriously because we are deeply concerned, not for God, but for those that try to mock Him. It would be more intelligent to stand on a golf course hill in Florida during a severe lightning storm and shake your fist at forked lightning—"God is not mocked. For whatever a man sows, that will he also reap."

Jodie Foster and God

I have heard it said many times, that the existence of God can't be proven. It is simply a matter of faith. I respectfully disagree. It is easy to prove the existence of God, absolutely, scientifically, 100%, without mentioning the Bible or exercising "faith."

On the July 7, 1997 airing of "Good Morning America" Foster was interviewed by co-anchor Charles Gibson about her then-upcoming movie *Contact*. The topic turned to the religious impacts of the movie and then to her religious beliefs.

At one point, she explained the "God of the gaps" concept, and that the "gaps" are continually getting tighter and tighter, and that we're running out of room for God as an explanation for the mystical. Gibson asked "Do you believe in God—I've never asked anyone this before?" Foster skirted the issue just a bit, referring to "fables" and "holy texts," insinuating a lack of credibility of them in her view. She also described her beliefs as similar to those of her character in the movie and that she can certainly never have proof of God's existence or non-existence.[2]

---

2 http://www.celebatheists.com/index.php?title=Jodie_Foster

She is further quoted as saying,

> "... how could you ask me to believe in God when there's absolutely no evidence that I can see? I do believe in the beauty and the awe-inspiring mystery of the science that's out there that we haven't discovered yet, that there are scientific explanations for phenomena that we call mystical because we don't know any better."[3]

We are often awed by the word "science." But the word simply means "knowledge," so I am going to give Miss Foster some knowledge that will show her how she can know for sure that God exists.

To have to do this is a little embarrassing. It's like having to explain that the sun exists, at noon on a warm sunny day. There may be a country somewhere that never sees the sun—every day is cloudy, but I would say to a man who lives there and denies that the sun exists, "Sir, where do you think sunlight comes from?"

I know that God exists because I have experienced the warmth and light of His love in my life, and I would say to those who are cut off from knowing Him by the clouds of their own sins, "Sir, where do you think life as we know it comes from?"

So let's roll back the clouds and look at proof that God exists, for those who are in the shadow of doubt.

When you look at a building, how can you know that there was a builder? You can't see him, hear him, touch, taste, or smell him. Here's how you can know. The *building* is absolute 100% scientific proof that there was a builder. You cannot have a building without a builder. You don't need faith to believe in a builder, all you need is eyes that can see and a brain that works.

When you look at a painting, how can you know if there was a painter? Here's how. The *painting* is absolute, one

---

3 http://www.celebatheists.com/index.php?title=Jodie_Foster

hundred percent scientific proof that there was a painter. Paintings don't happen by themselves.

Creation is absolute, one hunderd percent scientific proof that there was a Creator. *Everything* made has a maker. Everything—your car, your house, your bike, computer, your camera, and the book you are holding. If you look closely, you will see the maker's mark somewhere on the publication. The publishers of the book want you to know they exist. Look at the spine and you will see their logo. If for some reason you want to peel it off and trash it, go ahead. It may give you some sort of personal satisfaction, but it doesn't change the fact that the book still had a publisher, and that you have knowledge of that.

So where's God's logo? It is stamped on your mind in the area we call the "conscience." The word *con* means "with," and *science* means "knowledge." The conscience tells you (among other things) that God, as your Maker, should be first in your life.

The existence of God is so self evident through creation the issue is intellectually embarrassing to have to point out.[4] So the logical question arises, if everything made has a maker, who made God?

He is eternal. That means He has neither beginning nor end. We think in terms of everything having a beginning and an end because we dwell in something called "time." Time is a dimension that God created and then subjected mankind to.

---

4 Charles Butts spent several years booking atheist Madelyn Murray O'Hair on radio talk shows in America so she could spread her vitriolic message of hatred against God, and now he's the religion editor for USA Radio Network in Dallas, Texas. This is what happened: "If you take a look at some of the scientific arguments, Ray Comfort came out with a Bible specifically for that kind of thing, and so when that came out I certainly examined that ... I finished reading the Bible and had decided that all the questions that could be answered had been answered, and I'd watched TV enough that I knew the sinner's prayer and I knelt in the living room of my home and accepted Jesus Christ as my savior. I have never, ever regretted it."

But He dwells in "eternity" where there is no time. That's why He called Himself "I AM." He just IS.

The existence of God is "axiomatic." It is self evident. To say there is no God is like standing outside on a warm sunny day and saying "There's no sun." It is academically insane. That's why the Bible says, "The fool has said in his heart 'There is no God.'"[5]

Why the Denial?

You proudly take a friend through your beautiful new house, and say, "Didn't the builder do a great job!" But instead of agreeing with you and giving him due praise, he says, "I don't believe that there was a builder!"

You are flabbergasted. You wonder if your friend has suddenly become mentally challenged. Or did he bang his head on an exposed beam? Why would he deny that there was a builder? Then a light goes on in your own head. You smile, and say, "So, there's some sort of problem between you and the builder, huh?" That's your only avenue of logical conclusion. There would be no other reason for an intelligent rational human being to suddenly abandon all logic and basic reasonableness and deny something so blatantly self-evident.

Therein lies the problem between the professing atheist and God. There is a state of enmity between them.[6] He does have a good reason for being *unreasonable.* He objects to the moral government of God. He says, "God, don't you tell me what to do with my life. I love my lust, my fornication, my adultery, and my pornography. It's my life and I will do what I want with it! I am therefore going to go to the extreme of denying your very existence. You don't exist, in my mind." And in so doing, he will bring upon himself what the Bible calls "swift destruction."

---

5 See Psalm 14:1

6 See Romans 8:7

In 1997, Oliver Stone[1] described himself as a practicing Buddhist. Specifically, he has said he followed the Tibetan branch of Buddhism. He was not born into Buddhism, but adopted the faith as an adult. His father was Jewish American. His mother was a French Catholic. Neither of Stone's parents were particularly religious. In fact, they raised him in neither Judaism nor Catholicism. He was raised as an Episcopalian and regularly attended Episcopalian church services and Sunday School as a youth. He thought of himself as a Protestant, but describes himself as not particularly religious while growing up.[2]

Then in July 2005, when asked if he was still a Buddhist, he told *The Austin Chronicle*:

---

1 Oliver Stone is an acclaimed Hollywood director and writer. He was born on September 15, 1946 in New York City. Stone studied Liberal Arts at Yale University but left after only one year. After a stint as an English teacher in South Vietnam and a trip to Mexico, Stone enlisted in the US army. It was 1967, and with the Vietnam War, Stone found himself again in Vietnam, this time taking part in active combat duty. He won awards for extraordinary acts of bravery under fire and used his experiences in the war as the basis for three of his most personal films. His Vietnam trilogy looked at the war from different points of view. *Platoon* (1986), *Born on the Fourth of July* (1989) and *Heaven and Earth* (1993) were all either semi-autobiographical or true stories.

2 Edward Lagrossa, "Stone Soul Booksigning" (interview with Oliver Stone), October 20, 1997, in *The Austin Chronicle*.

"Yes. I'm a practicing Buddhist or a student of it, whatever you want to call it … it's a state of trying to reach enlightenment." When asked if he brought his religion to work by making it part of his films, he said, "Trying to. It may strike you as bizarre, but it's closely allied. My work is mostly about the spirit life."

> "I'm a practicing Buddhist or a student of it, whatever you want to call it."
> –Oliver Stone

When asked "Which of your other movies would you say is more exemplary of your inner philosophy?" He said, "*Heaven and Earth*. The beauty of the woman, LeLy, a true story. Her ability to forgive her enemies. To transcend her pain. I think that is a great ending. It's a great moral. She was a Buddhist and she converted me to the Vietnamese church, and then I went on to the Tibetan.[3]"

In an interview with Tom Allen and Tim Rice entitled "Oliver Stone wants more," Oliver Stone was asked if he was raised "Catholic or Jewish or neither?" He answered:

"Neither. I was raised Protestant. I went to Sunday school in New York and I was a Protestant, so called, although I don't think I was really very religious. He was asked about one of his movies (*Heaven and Earth*) "Why in the film you come across as being hostile to Catholicism." He said, "Hostile is not the right word. Any Buddhist would tell you that any spiritual life that works for you is good, be it Muslim, Hindu, Catholic or any other. Whatever brings you closer to an awareness of your intrinsic nature is good. And they've been highly tolerant of other faiths. I think the point I was trying to make was that LeLy was puzzled and I am puzzled by the Christian insistence on original sin and insistence on suffering. If you notice, all the imagery or most of the imagery in the Catholic icons is people who have been martyred, people with nails through their bodies.

3 http://weeklywire.com/ww/10-20-97/austin_screens_feature4.html; viewed 1 July 2005

The Christ figure himself as I showed in the movie briefly is a figure of suffering. And it reflects Tommy Lee Jones' response to life, whereas in contrast, LeLy's response to suffering is not to martyr herself but to change. I think Buddhism offers a certain flexibility, an ability to change that Tommy Lee does not have in the movie."[4]

James Cameron Discovers Ice on the Sun

Another big name Hollywood director is James Cameron.[5] In March 2007, he announced something that he no doubt hoped would go down as well as *Titanic*. It *was* big news. When Cameron (with less subtlety than his Hollywood counterparts) attempted to sink Christianity by producing "the bones of Jesus," even *Time* Magazine couldn't help but use the word "showman" and be reminded of Hollywood fiction:

> Ever the showman (why does this remind me of the impresario in another movie, *King Kong*, whose hubris blinds him to the dangers of an angry and very large ape?), Cameron is holding a New York press conference on Monday at which he will reveal three coffins, supposedly those of Jesus of Nazareth, his mother Mary and Mary Magdalene.[6]

Ironically, it's not the first time the imaginative director has tried to help us understand the Bible. A year earlier he produced a documentary that made big news in England:

---

4 http://www.moviemaker.com/issues/12/stone.html; viewed 1 July 2005

5 James Francis Cameron is a successful three-time Academy Award winning director noted for his action/science fiction films. He directed Titanic, which went on to become the top-grossing film of all time, with a worldwide gross of over $1.8 billion; he also created *The Terminator* franchise.

6 http://time-blog.com/middle_east/2007/02/jesus_tales_from_the_crypt.html

> The greatest story ever told has acquired a Hollywood twist. James Cameron, the director of *Titanic*, is the executive producer of a new documentary that claims to have uncovered fresh evidence confirming one of the most dramatic episodes in the Old Testament—the parting of the Red Sea and the Jewish exodus from Egypt. …Cameron believes the parting of the Red Sea may have been a tsunami that destroyed the pharaoh's army as it pursued the escaping Jews. The documentary claims the episode occurred not at the Red Sea but at the smaller Sea of Reeds, a marshy area at the northern end of the Gulf of Suez. An underwater earthquake may have released poisonous gases that turned the waters red.[7]

So the opening of the Red Sea wasn't a spontaneous miracle of God. It was a well-timed earthquake and tsunami. Thanks Mr. Cameraman for framing that for us and for putting the issue in focus.

So, how can Christians be *sure* that James Cameron is wrong? There are a couple of things in life of which I am truly sure. The first is that the sun is hot. I may be wrong, but everything around me—my natural senses, my life's experience, science, etc.—comes together to tell me that the sun is very hot. The second thing of which I am sure is that Jesus Christ is the Son of God, that He suffered and died for me, rose again on the third day, and that "God has appointed Him to judge the quick and the dead."

The thought that someone has found the bones of Jesus doesn't even come up to being a very bad joke. It would be more credible for Mr. Cameron to produce a documentary telling us that the sun is made of ice. He could perhaps have it aired on the Comedy Channel.

Why am I so sure that Jesus Christ is the Son of God? Because He transformed my life. He made me a brand new person on the inside. The first time I was born, it was radical.

---

7 http://www.timesonline.co.uk/tol/news/world/article601300.ece

I didn't exist, then I did. When I was "born again," it was just as radical. To understand that, you have to look to the Law of Moses for a moment. It says, "You shall not commit adultery," but this Jesus of whom Mr. Cameron speaks, said, "But I say to you, whoever looks upon a woman to lust after her, has committed adultery already with her in his heart." That's the standard humanity will be judged by, and I don't know about you, but that would leave me guilty, and the Bible warns that it would put me in Hell—for eternity. That's why I need a Savior, who took my punishment, and then rose from the dead to give me peace with God.

It is because of that cross that I am forgiven, and it was the ultimate happy day, "when Jesus washed, when Jesus washed, Jesus washed my sins away." That's the only hill I will die on ... *that's because One has already died on a hill for me.*

Evolution and Hollywood

George Lucas shot from comparative obscurity into Hollywood with *Star Wars*. He said that he produced the movie to cause young people in particular to think about God.[1] But the deity he believes in isn't the God of the Bible:

"The way I define intelligent design is that when people started out we wanted to make sense of the world we lived in, so we created stories about how things worked. The end result, obviously, was to create spirits or gods of one form or another that functioned beyond our knowledge—that would explain why the sun went down at night, why babies were born, and that sort of thing. You didn't have to explain it yourself. You just had to say, 'Well, there's something there that explains all that, and if you just have faith in that, you'll be fine.'

"That's always the way it's been. But I think that God gave us a brain, and that it's the only thing we have to survive. All life forms have some advantage, some trick, some claw, some camouflage, some poison, some speed, something to help them survive. We've got a brain. Therefore it's our duty to use our brain. Because we have an intellect, part of what we do is try to understand the intelligent design. Everything we don't know is intelligent design. Everything we do know is science.

1 See *What Hollywood Believes* by Ray Comfort

"In other words, evolution is a product of intelligent design. There's absolutely no conflict between Darwinism and God's design for the universe—if you believe that it's God's design. The problem for me is that I see a very big difference between the Bible and God. And the problem they're getting into now is that they're trying to understand intelligent design through the Bible, not through God. Our job is to find all the intelligent design, and figure out how He did everything, and I think that's consistent with science."[2]

> "The problem for me is that I see a very big difference between the Bible and God."
> –George Lucas

George Lucas is correct about there being a problem, if I embrace evolution. The problem is that I then *have* to reject the Bible. That's a dilemma because the Bible is the explanation of how the Creator created this intelligently designed creation of which we are a part.

Evolution and the Bible are *incompatible*. The Scriptures says that God caused every animal to bring forth "after its own kind"[3] (dogs don't have kittens, fish don't turn into sheep, etc., no matter how long they are left). There is micro-evolution within each species, but they stay within the same kind.

He also made man in *His* image. We are also told in Scripture that there is one kind of flesh of man and another of the beasts.[4] They are not one in the same. One didn't evolve into another.

If you, like George Lucas, have faith in the theory of evolution, please consider the following information from

---

2 http://www.boston.com/ae/movies/lucas_interview/

3 See Genesis chapter one.

4 "All flesh is not the same flesh: but there is one kind of flesh of men, another flesh of beasts, another of fishes, and another of birds" (1 Corinthians 15:39).

some experts who have done their duty and used the brain that God gave them:

- "Evolution is a fairytale for grown-ups. This theory has helped nothing in the progress of science. It is useless." Professor Louis Bounoure, Director of Research, National Center of Scientific Research, *The Advocate*, March 8, 1984.
- "Paleontologists have discovered a new skeleton in the closet of human ancestry that is likely to force science to revise, if not scrap, current theories of human origins. Reuters reported that the discovery left scientists of human evolution ... confused, saying, 'Lucy may not even be a direct human ancestor after all." *USA Today,* March 21, 2001.
- "I myself am convinced that the theory of evolution, especially the extent to which it has been applied, will be one of the great jokes in the history books of the future." Malcolm Muggeridge (British philosopher), *The Advocate*, March 8 1984.
- "Scientists who go about teaching that evolution is a fact of life are great con-men, and the story they are telling may be the greatest hoax ever. In explaining evolution, we do not have one iota of fact." Dr. T. N. Tahmisian (Atomic Energy Commission), *The Fresno Bee,* August 20, 1959.
- "Scientists concede that their most cherished theories are based on embarrassingly few fossil fragments and that huge gaps exist in the fossil record." *Time* magazine, Nov. 7, 1977.
- "As by this theory, innumerable transitional forms must have existed. Why do we not find them embedded in the crust of the earth?" Charles Darwin, *Evolution or Creation*, p.139.
- "If pressed about man's ancestry, I would have to unequivocally say that all we have is a huge question mark." Richard Leakey, paleo-anthropologist.

- "The more scientists have searched for the transitional forms that lie between species, the more they have been frustrated." *Newsweek*, November 3, 1980.
- "Often a cold shudder has run through me, and I have asked myself whether I may have not devoted myself to a fantasy." Charles Darwin, *Life and Letters*, 1887, Vol. 2, p. 229.
- "I would rather believe in fairy tales than in such wild speculation." Sir Ernest Chain, co-holder of 1945 Nobel Prize for developing penicillin (*The Life of Ernest Chain*, Ronald W. Clark, pp. 147-148).
- "The main problem in reconstructing the origins of man is lack of fossil evidence: all there is could be displayed on a dinner table." *New Scientist*, 20 May, 1982.

In 1999, a Chinese farmer glued together the head and body of a primitive bird and the tail and hind limbs of a dromaeosaur dinosaur, and completely fooled the worldwide scientific community into thinking that they had found the "missing link" between carnivorous dinosaurs and modern birds. [*National Geographic Magazine*, Vol. 196, No. 5, November, 1999]. Named Archaeoraptor, "this fossil find constitutes the most recent evolution fraud ... that we know of. Storrs L. Olson of the Smithsonian Institution said, "National Geographic has reached an all-time low for engaging in sensationalistic, unsubstantiated, tabloid journalism."

A transitional form (or a "missing link") is an example of one species "evolving" into another species. Excited scientists thought they had found one when they discovered "Archaeopteryx." The fossil led to the theory that the dinosaurs did not become extinct, but rather all turned into birds. The Field Museum in Chicago displayed what was believed to be an archaeopteryx fossil on October 4-19, 1997. It was hailed as "Archaeopteryx: The Bird That Rocked the World." However, Dr. Alan Feduccia (evolutionary biologist at the University of North Carolina), said, "Paleontologists have tried to turn Archaeopteryx into an earth-bound, feathered dinosaur. But it's not. It is a bird, a perching bird. And no amount of 'paleo-babble' is going to change that." [*Science*, February 5, 1993.]

So here's a challenge for the evolution believer. Charles Darwin said, "As by this theory, innumerable transitional forms must have existed. Why do we not find them embedded in the crust of the earth?" The reason we can't find them *is because they don't exist.*

I will give $10,000 to the first person who can prove to me that they have found a genuine living transitional form (a lizard that produced a bird, or a dog that produced kittens, or a sheep that produced a chicken, or even an Archaeopteryx—a dinosaur that produced a bird[5]).

Species do not cross, no matter how long you leave them. The whole of creation is proof that evolution is truly "a fairytale for grownups." The fairytale of evolution is another pathetic effort to get rid of the problem of God and His Moral Law. The god of evolution, like the millions of gods of wood and stone, doesn't exist.[6]

A Problem for Hollywood

Here though is an ethical problem for Hollywood's evolution advocates. The essence of the theory is the philosophy of "survival of the fittest." At the same time as being Darwinists, many of Hollywood's elite are anti-war. But if we are just animals, war between animal nations is simply a matter of the fit surviving by killing off the weaker animal nations. The Catholic murders of the crusades and the horrific burning of innocent people during the Inquisition were simply examples of the fit surviving.

---

5 See www.IntelligentDesignversusEvolution.com for details.

6 "For Hinduism there may be millions of gods!...however, **these gods are not God, they cannot make stars, nor roses, nor human hearts**... they should not be adored." http://www.religion-cults.com/Eastern/Hinduism/hindu4.htm "It has been said that Hinduism is a religion of 330 million Hinduism gods." http://www.allaboutreligion.org/hinduism-gods-faq.htm

Darwin, the Racist

One of the most important yet least-known aspects of Darwin is his racism:

> Darwin regarded white Europeans as more "advanced" than other human races. While Darwin presumed that man evolved from ape-like creatures, he surmised that some races developed more than others and that the latter still bore simian features. In his book, *The Descent of Man*, which he published after *The Origin of Species*, he boldly commented on "the greater differences between men of distinct races."[7]

In his book, Charles Darwin held blacks and Australian Aborigines to be equal to gorillas and then inferred that these would be "done away with" by the "civilized races" in time. If any Christian appeared on television and said that he believed that black people were on the same level as gorillas, he would be labeled as a hate-filled racist—a bigoted fundamentalist. But Darwin is venerated by millions. His words are believed and preached as if they were gospel truth by his blind followers. Look at the racism of the prophet Charles Darwin as he predicts the future:

> At some future period, not very distant as measured by centuries, the civilized races of man will almost certainly exterminate and replace the savage races throughout the world. At the same time the anthropomorphous apes ... will no doubt be exterminated. The break between man and his nearest allies will then be wider, for it will intervene in a more civilized state, as we may hope, even than the Caucasian, and some ape as low as baboon, instead of as now between the negro or Australian and the gorilla.[8]

---

7 Benjamin Farrington, *What Darwin Really Said.* London: Sphere Books, 1971, pp. 54-56.

8 Charles Darwin, *The Descent of Man*, 2nd edition, New York, A L. Burt Co., 1874, p. 178.

Darwin's close friend Professor Adam Sedgwick was one of the people who saw what dangers the theory of evolution would give rise to in the future. He remarked, after reading and digesting *The Origin of Species* that "if this book were to find general public acceptance, it would bring with it a brutalization of the human race such as it had never seen before.[9]

Politically Correct Hollywood

It's ironic that Hollywood is so politically correct, because it embraces a philosophy of life that, at its core, is racist and promotes racism. Look at how it has worked into the mindset of Madonna:

> Madonna was quoted as saying she would be unlikely to choose a black partner again. Claiming to have been mistreated when she dated black men, she allegedly said: "Maybe a lot of it has to do with the fact that they haven't had the same chances as we white people have had to be educated or exposed to things that make you more evolved."[10]

---

9 A.E. Wilder-Smith, *Man's Origin Man's Destiny*, The Word for Today Publishing, 1993, p.166 "Weikart concludes that Darwinism played a key role not only in the rise of eugenics, but also in euthanasia, infanticide, abortion, and racial extermination, all ultimately embraced by the Nazis. He convincingly makes the disturbing argument that Hitler built his view of ethics on Darwinian principles rather than nihilistic ones." http://web.csustan.edu/History/Faculty/Weikart/FromDarwintoHitler.htm "I don't claim that Darwin and his theory of evolution brought on the holocaust; but I cannot deny that the theory of evolution, and the atheism it engendered, led to the moral climate that made a holocaust possible" Jewish scholar Edward Simon, *Another Side to the Evolution Problem*, Jewish Press, Jan. 7,1983, pp.248.

10 *The Daily Telegraph*, Sydney, 15 October 1996.

Inherit the Wind

You may have seen Hollywood's much heralded movie *Inherit the Wind*, starring Spencer Tracy and Fredric March, directed by Stanley Kramer. Here is a typical review of the film:

> *Inherit the Wind* (1960) portrays, in partly fictionalized form, the famous and dramatic courtroom "Monkey Trial" battle (in the sultry summer of 1925 in Dayton, Tennessee) between two famous lawyers (Clarence Darrow and William Jennings Bryan) who volunteered to heatedly argue both sides of the case (over twelve days, including two weekends).
>
> The story centers around the issue of evolution vs. creationism, in the prosecution of 24-year-old Dayton High School mathematics teacher and sports coach—and substitute science teacher—John T. Scopes for violating state law (the 1925 Butler Act) by teaching Darwin's theory of evolution in a state-funded school. The film's title was taken from the Biblical book of *Proverbs 11:29*: "He that troubleth his own house shall inherit the wind."[1]

Notice that the reviewer rightly says that this movie portrays the historical trial "in partly fictionalized form." In their fictionalizing of the movie, Hollywood actually perverted historical truth:

---

1 http://www.filmsite.org/inhe.html

Throughout the film William Jennings Bryan is portrayed as pompous, stupid, intolerant, hypocritical, insincere and as a glutton. As the trial progresses, Bryan becomes virtually obsessed with his mission of prosecuting John Scopes and keeping the theory of evolution out of the schools. Even Bryan's wife gradually comes to realize that her husband is a zealot and seems to regret that she didn't get to know Clarence Darrow a little better in their younger years. In the movie, Bryan's reputation as an orator is called into question, and he is portrayed as a strutting and arrogant sounding "flim-flam man" whose style and tedious sense of humor appeals only to ignorant folks (the slow-witted Christian Fundamentalists). It is hardly possible to watch the film without developing a sense of contempt for William Jennings Bryan and the Christian Fundamentalists who somehow find something to admire in the man.

However, in his book *The Great Monkey Trial*, Sprague de Camp[2] repudiates Bryan's conservative Christianity and misses no opportunity to be critical of his scientific views and yet, honesty compelled him to give Bryan credit for at least some of his undeniable virtues:

"As a speaker, Bryan radiated good humored sincerity. Few who heard him could help liking him. In personality he was forceful, energetic, and opinionated but genial, kindly, generous, likable and charming. He showed a praise worthy tolerance towards those who disagreed with him. Bryan was the greatest American orator of his time and perhaps any time."[3]

---

2 *The Great Monkey Trial* is a 1968 book on the Scopes Trial by L. Sprague de Camp, first published in hardcover by Doubleday. This history of the trial was based on the memoirs of John T. Scopes, the archives of the A.C.L.U., assorted newspaper files, correspondence and interviews with dozens of those present at the trial, books and magazine articles written on the trial (including the official record of the trial in the Rhea County Courthouse), and two visits to Dayton.

3 L Sprague deCamp, page 37.

This is obviously not the man portrayed in the film, but de Camp's description of Bryan's character is entirely consistent with the major biographies of Bryan's life.

None the less, many of Bryan's enemies insisted that, regardless of his many virtues, he was ignorant and even dangerous when it came to scientific or factual matters. The historical record does not support this accusation:

> Bryan was not just a "commoner," as even he liked to portray himself, but was also an immensely productive and progressive politician who was the recognized leader of the Democratic party for thirty years and was three times nominated by his Party as their candidate for President of the United States ... Bryan appealed to a broad cross section of people including those whose political views were decidedly liberal. Clarence Darrow himself twice campaigned for Bryan when he ran for President of the United States. Many of the "progressives" who supported Bryan, however, came to despise him for his outspoken Christian convictions, particularly when he dared to speak out against Darwinism.
>
> The conservative Christian people of Dayton, Tennessee, are portrayed as ignorant, closed minded, discourteous and even threatening towards the lawyers for the defense, the news media and outsiders in general.
>
> However, the transcript of the Scopes trial shows this to be precisely the opposite of the truth:
>
> Darrow: "I don't know as I was ever in a community in my life where my religious ideas differed as widely from the great mass as I have found them since I have been in Tennessee. Yet I came here a perfect stranger and I can say what I have said before that I have not found upon anybody's part—any citizen here in this town or outside—the slightest discourtesy. I have been treated better, kindlier and more hospitably than I fancied would have been the case in the north." (transcript, pages 225-226).[4]

---

4 http://www.pathlights.com/InherittheWind.htm

Inherit the Wind was honored by Hollywood with four Academy Award nominations, but won no Oscars. The tragedy is that few people understand the way in which the movie is fictionalized, and it has therefore been very effective in furthering Hollywood's agenda—to make Christians look foolish, mock their beliefs, and keep this blind world from trusting in the God of the Bible.

Global Warming

Many actors have openly spoken against those who disregard the thought that the planet is warming, and how this increase in temperature will have terrible repercussions for future generations. But if evolution is true, and evolution has been responsible for getting us this far, won't evolution also fix global warming without our help?

If evolution was the one in charge of placing the sun where it is, and for creating the delicate amount of oxygen in the air, for the amazing balance of the weather patterns, for the regular tidal systems governed by the earth's gravitational pull and the earth's distance from the moon, we should stand in awe of its incredible ability. If evolution is responsible for creating the unspeakably amazing human eye with its 137,000,000 light sensitive cells, surely fixing global warming will be a piece of cake. Yet believers almost live in a panic. It seems their faith in the ability of evolution to fix anything after doing such a wonderful job in the beginning is a little lacking.

Someone once said that we are on a huge spinning ball of dirt, screaming through space at thousands of miles an hour. If no one is in control (i.e., we all came about as some random evolutionary accident), we are in big trouble. Then again, with all the evil in the world, if Someone *is* in control, we are in big trouble.

Or perhaps, like Oliver Stone and many other celebrities, you believe in God but He's not the God of the Bible, and you see Him more as a God of love and mercy. Okay. Let's go with that for a minute. The God of the Bible speaks of a day of Judgment, and besides that, He told Joshua to kill the Canaanites—every man, woman and child. You look at other things He sanctions in the Bible, and they deeply offend you. To be frank, He is a wrath-filled tyrant. Your God would never do that. Perhaps the world's most famous atheist, Richard Dawkins feels similarly:

> The God of the Old Testament is arguably the most unpleasant character in all of fiction. Jealous and proud of it; a petty, unjust, unforgiving control-freak; a vindictive, bloodthirsty ethnic-cleanser; a misogynistic homophobic racist, infanticidal, genocidal, filicidal, pestilential, megalo-maniacal...[5]

Perhaps you have asked Christians about this tyrannical God, and they quote Bible verses such as, "All of God's judgments are righteous and true altogether." They say that they don't understand some things, and that they simply trust God, and one day they will comprehend difficulties such as these. The explanation doesn't satisfy you. That's the reason you reject Christianity.

Here now is a thought for you. Why does the God you believe in allow children to die of cancer? He does. Every year, thousands of young children suffer and die of the terrible disease. He also allows 40,000 children to die of starvation every 24 hours. That's approximately how many die every day throughout the world. Your God allows that. He also allowed Nazi Germany to slaughter millions. How do you explain that? Why does He allow hurricanes and tornados to kill people? Is your God "God" or isn't He? Or is He impotent? Then he's not God. If He's the Creator, He made all things, and He therefore has total power and control. Why then doesn't He do something to stop the suffering?

Perhaps you say that He is in control, but He has removed His hand from humanity. Are you then saying that He's aloof

---

5 Richard Dawkins, "The God Delusion," Houghton Miffin, (2006).

from human suffering—He doesn't care? Then He's not a God of love and mercy. Your God has a heart of stone. And therein lies the problem with your god. He's an idol. He doesn't exist. He is a figment of the imagination.

Man is as attracted to the sin of "idolatry" as flees to a dog. That's why he so quickly jumped onto evolution. Idolatry (making up our own god) is attractive because our own concept of God is shaped in our minds so that we feel comfortable with Him. I had my own comfortable concept of God before I was converted.

Hollywood has its own concept of God. That's why they have no problem mocking Him with their movies:

> Modern-day Hollywood theology, you might say, began with *Oh God!*, a movie comedy that gave us the ancient and affable George Burns portraying a kindly Almighty in a baseball cap. The flick was a hit. Screenwriters had stumbled on a transcendent formula for success: Make God non-threatening, nondenominational and, if possible, hilarious. Remember, this was 1977. The nation was weary after Vietnam, Watergate, assassinations and other social convulsions. Religious pluralism was on the rise. We needed a reassuring word from a wisecracking Creator.[6]

The truth is, when we stand in moral judgment over Almighty God and accuse Him of sin, it's because we have a knowledge of right and wrong. We are moral beings, and we get that from being created in His image. What we must do is turn that moral spotlight upon ourselves. The cold hard fact that the best of us is at best a devious criminal tends to put our judgments into perspective, despite the difficulties in the Bible.

However, our salvation (contrary to common belief) is independent of our acceptance of the Bible. We will look at this fact in the next chapter.

---

6 http://archives.umc.org/interior.asp?ptid=2&mid=2836

Self Made Star

Bruce Willis has no need for God in his life. He is shaping up to his movie image. He's a self-made, confident, self-satisfied man:

> "I was surprised how seamless it was to turn 40. I have a lot of things going for me. I'm in the best shape of my life. I've got a couple dollars in my pocket. I have a great family and great friends. Forty feels great. In my heart I'm like 22 anyway. I believe that around me are things I pulled into my orbit, things I made happen. I'll take responsibility for them—it's not like God put them there. I feel good about what's around me because I worked hard for it."[1]

As we have seen, George Lucas isn't so independent. He sees the necessity for some sort of faith in some sort of God, anything but the God of the Bible. This is because he isn't convinced that the Bible is the Word of the Creator. If the Bible proved itself to indeed be the Word of God, then perhaps he would rest his faith on it.

There are many people who are convinced that the Christian faith stands or falls on whether or not the Bible is divine. This is believed by both Christians and skeptics. Christians argue with the world about the authenticity of Scripture.

---

1 http://www.playboy.com/arts-entertainment/features/bruce-willis/04.html

They appeal to people's intellect by pointing to the Dead Sea scrolls, to prophecy, to the Bible's historical accuracy, etc., to establish its divine inspiration in the minds of an unbelieving world. This was why James Cameron knew he would make big news when he came up with what he said were the bones of Jesus. If they were authentic, the New Testament in particular was unreliable, and therefore Christianity comes crumbling down like the Walls of Jericho.

> "I believe that around me are things I pulled into my orbit, things I made happen.
> I'll take responsibility for them—it's not like God put them there."
> –Bruce Willis

But if the Christian faith rested entirely on the New Testament's inspiration, upon what did the faith of the early Church rest? The New Testament didn't exist in the early part of the first century, and yet multitudes were soundly converted to Jesus Christ. This was because they simply heard the *spoken* message of the gospel, repented and trusted in the risen Savior. Jesus Christ truly was and is still the *foundation* of the Church, and, as the Church is made up of believers, the foundation for each believer is simply faith in His person. He is the Rock upon which I stand. I am complete in Him with or without a New Testament.

However, since the compilation of the New Testament, the populous' ability to read and the advent of the printing press, we now have access to the Word of God, and it has become an integral part of our faith. But it wasn't always so.

To illustrate this important point, let's put a modern convert into the "dilemma" of not having access to, or even knowing about, the New Testament.

This Day Was Different

Two men are in a Russian dungeon. One is a Christian who has been horribly tortured for his faith. As he lies dying in his cell, he shares his faith with his unbelieving cell mate.

The other prisoner is a bitter man who so despised Christians, he hadn't spoken to him since they were forced to share the tiny cell. But this day was different. He listens intently to the dying man's words, because of the fact that he is on his deathbed. Through parched lips the Christian whispers the Ten Commandments, showing sin to be very serious in the sight of God.

The man becomes deeply concerned as his conscience begins to bear witness to what he is hearing.[2] He begins to see that because he has broken God's Law, the wrath of this just God is upon him.[3] There is no talk of a god-shaped vacuum, a wonderful plan, or any benefits of faith in Jesus during this life. How could the Christian talk of a wonderful plan that so many speak of while he lies dying because he has been beaten for his faith? The cell mate simply hears that he is a desperately wicked criminal who needs forgiveness from the God he has greatly angered. Then he hears the pure Gospel of the love of God in Christ, and of the necessity of repentance and faith. He hears of the One who can wash him clean. It answers his problem of coming wrath. The Christian then pleads with him to repent, breaths his last, and passes into eternity.

The prisoner is left alone in the cold cell. He is shaken by what he has just heard. He falls to his knees on the hard floor and trembles before God. He can hardly lift his head because of the weight of his sins. In humble contrition, he openly confesses his many transgressions against God's Law. He pleads for mercy, repents, and places his entire trust in Jesus Christ for his eternal salvation. He has no Bible. He has no fellowship. He has no one to follow him up. He is entirely alone.

The next day he wakens while still lying on the floor. As he opens his tired eyes, something is different. Radically different. There's a song in his heart. It's not a "song" that he could sing,

---

2 Romans 2:15

3 Romans 4:15

but it's some sort of a joy that he can hardly express. He also has a sense of peace that is beyond his comprehension. He has never felt these emotions before, and what is mystifying is that he has no reason to feel this joy. He is tired, alone, and hungry, in a cold dungeon. He also notices that he is no longer ashamed to lift his head to the heavens. In fact, he *wants* to speak to Him in prayer. But more than that, he has an overwhelming desire to please God more than anything else in his life. He even noticed that his nagging conscience was silenced and *any* sense of guilt about any of his past sins was gone. He was amazed at what he had experienced. Again, nothing like this had ever happened before—not for a fleeting moment in his bitter godless years. Never. God was the last thing on his mind.

He then looked at the lifeless body of the cell mate he once despised, and longed to speak with him. He wanted to ask for his forgiveness. He wanted to talk about the God that made Himself known to him; the God that forgave him for his sins … the God that loved him enough to send His Son to die for him.

This was more than some sort of subjective experience. He was a brand new person with a new heart and new desires. Tears filled his eyes as he thought of the cross of Jesus Christ. Oh that wonderful cross! Jesus of Nazareth suffered and died for him! He defeated death. His heart almost burst with joy.

After five years of solitary confinement, our prisoner has grown in grace. He has matured in the faith. He has preached the gospel to hardened guards. He told them of the standard of perfection with which God would judge them, opening up the Ten Commandments. He has faithfully shared the reality of Judgment Day and the terrors of an eternal Hell. He preached Christ crucified for the sin of the world, and the necessity of repentance and faith. The guards taunt him regularly, and now and then beat him. He, in return, prays earnestly for their salvation. He also prays for the salvation of his family, and for the world. He continually worships God and lives a life of holiness, free from sin, trusting minute by minute in the finished work of Calvary's cross.

Notice that he is strong in his faith *and he has not yet even seen a Bible or spoken to another Christian.* His faith rests on the fact that God made him a new creature, wrote His Law on his heart and caused him to walk in His statutes.[4] He is a new person, a "new man, which after God is created in righteousness and true holiness."[5] Old things passed away and all things became new.[6] He was born of God.[7] The New Testament didn't convert him. It was the spoken *gospel* that was the power of God unto salvation.[8] Neither did the New Testament spiritually feed him. His faith wasn't in the Scriptures or a church or another person. It wasn't in his good works or in his religion. It was the fact that he was a new creature that convinced him of the reality of God.

The Explanation Book

One day, a sympathetic guard slips the prisoner a New Testament. The prisoner doesn't even know what it is. All he knows is that it is a book about the Savior he loves. He carefully opens its sacred pages for the first time in his life, and for the next few days he drinks in truths about Jesus of Nazareth. Does his faith stand or fall on the New Testament truths? No. His faith was strong before he even opened the Scriptures. However, his faith is strengthened by the fact that this 2,000-year-old book *confirmed his experience.* It brought him comfort.[9] It explained why he suddenly longed for Christian fellowship.[10] It spoke directly to his peace that

---

4 Ezekiel 11:19

5 Ephesians 4:24

6 2 Corinthians 5:17

7 John 1:12-13

8 Romans 1:16

9 Romans 15:4

10 1 John 3:14

passed all understanding,[11] and it spoke about why he loved Jesus Christ (whom he had never seen) and why he had an unspeakable joy that bubbled within him.[12] It addressed the fact that he was born again[13], a new creature in Christ,[14] and why it was that he continually thought of Jesus of Nazareth[15] and the cross.[16]

How do I know that Christianity is true? Is it dependent on the inspiration of the New Testament? No. It doesn't rise or fall on that fact. The New Testament simply confirms my experience and provides milk and meat to help me to grow in my faith.[17] Christianity isn't true because the New Testament confirms it. The believer believes it's true because he trusts in the Living God. The Moral Law put him at the edge of the plane door, staring in horror at a ten thousand foot drop. The gospel perfectly addressed that problem. I am persuaded that it's true because it answered my need of a Savior.

This is good news for Christianity. It means that we don't need to try and convince the world of the divine inspiration of the Scriptures. It means that when a skeptic says that the Bible is filled with mistakes, we need not spend our time trying to defend it. If we look at the preaching of Jesus and the apostles, we don't see them trying to convince the world of anything but their danger, and the only way to do that is to lovingly talk about things they disdain—of sin, righteousness and judgment.

A. W. Tozer insightfully addresses the error of sharing our faith by appealing to the intellect as a means of persuasion:

---

11 Philippians 4:7

12 1 Peter 1:8

13 John 3:3-7, 1 Peter 1:23

14 2 Corinthians 5:17

15 John 16:14

16 Galatians 6:14

17 1 Peter 2:2

Our trouble is that we are trying to confirm the truth of Christianity by an appeal to external evidence. We are saying, "Well, look at this fellow. He can throw a baseball farther than anybody else and he is a Christian, therefore Christianity must be true." "Here is a great statesman who believes the Bible. Therefore, the Bible must be true." We quote Daniel Webster, or Roger Bacon. We write books to show that some scientist believed in Christianity; therefore, Christianity must be true. We are all the way out on the wrong track, brother! That is not New Testament Christianity at all. That is a pitiful, whimpering, drooling appeal to the flesh. That never was the testimony of the New Testament, never the way God did things—never! You might satisfy the intellects of men by external evidences, and Christ did, I say, point to external evidence when He was here on the earth. But He said, "I am sending you something better. I am taking Christian apologetics out of the realm of logic and putting it into the realm of life. I am proving My deity, and My proof will not be an appeal to a general or a prime minister. The proof lies in an invisible, unseen but powerful energy that visits the human soul when the gospel is preached—the Holy Spirit!

So what do we say to a man who says that he is earnestly seeking for the truth? Do you try and convince him that the Bible is filled with incredible prophecies, and scientific truths, that great statesman and presidents believed the Scriptures. No. We simply put him into the dilemma of having to face a holy God after he dies. If he says things like, "How do I know the Bible is true? It was changed by so-and-so in the fourth century," tell him that his faith is misdirected. He is believing history books, written by the pen of fallible men, when all he needs to do is listen to his God-given conscience. He needs to believe its accusations under the light of the Law. He needs to believe the gospel because it is the only hope he has of escaping a very real Hell.

Therein lies the problem with so many in Hollywood who have some sort of semblance of Christianity. Many have become disillusioned with Catholicism, or they have seen through the horrible hypocrisy and shallowness of so much Christian television. The problem is that they have never been given the pure gospel from the lips of a dying man. They have been fed dead religion or a false gospel that promises a wonderful plan, happiness and prosperity. But Christianity isn't like a Hollywood marriage. There's no prenuptial agreement. It's not an experiment to see if it works. It's a complete surrender of the will.

Think of a good marriage. Both parties have laid down their will at the altar. The husband has said, "There is no one else. I have turned from my flirtatious lifestyle. You are my true love. I surrender my heart to you." That's the essence of conversion.

This is why a Christian will not waver for a moment if Hollywood produced what it believed was evidence that the New Testament is completely erroneous. Nor would he waver in the slightest if they came up with bones that *proved* to be that of a 33-year-old carpenter from Nazareth, who was crucified and had "I am Jesus of Nazareth" engraved into the skull.

Natural Made Killers

After the Columbine school massacre of thirteen people, Leonardo DiCaprio solemnly vowed never to star in another violent movie. Just after the violent murders, the *U.K. Mirror* reported:

> Hollywood star Leonardo DiCaprio has renounced violent films after one of his early movies was linked to the Columbine school massacre. The actor has told aides he no longer wants to be considered for parts in any productions featuring death and destruction. The 'Titanic' star has been caught up in the wave of revulsion sweeping America after the slaughter of twelve pupils and a teacher at the school in the Denver suburb of Littleton. In the 1995 drama 'The Basketball Diaries,' DiCaprio played a teenage heroin addict who gunned down his teacher and classmates. His twisted screen character wore a full-length trench coat— just like those worn by Trenchcoat Mafia murderers Eric Harris and Dylan Klebold who carried out the classroom killings two weeks ago. The parents of three pupils shot dead in 1997 in a school in Kentucky have already sued the makers of *The Basketball Diaries* for $100 million. The families of the thirteen Columbine victims are expected to follow suit, insisting the film inspired teenage misfits Harris and Klebold to mount their terrible attack. Worried British video distributors had the entire classroom killing sequence

cut from the film rather than risk sparking copycat murders in the U.K.[1]

Susan Sarandon warned:

> Movies are important; and they're dangerous because we're the keepers of the dreams. You go into a little dark room and become incredibly vulnerable. On the one hand, all your perspectives can be challenged. You can feel something you couldn't feel normally. [They] can encourage you to be the protagonist in your own life. On the other hand, [they] can completely misshape you.[2]

So why then hasn't Hollywood stopped making violent movies? Director Francis Ford Coppola reveals why:

> "I made the most vulgar, entertaining, actionful, sense-a-ramic, give them a thrill every five minutes, sex, violence, humor, because I want people to come see it."[3]

After Columbine, Hollywood didn't change its agenda of violence, even in the face of these massive law suits. It has the world's best lawyers and the money to defend itself. It knows that we are vulnerable, but it also knows that we will pay up at the box office.

On April 30, 1981, John Hinckley Jr. shot President Ronald Reagan. "Hinckley said he was trying to copy Robert De Niro's character in the movie *Taxi Driver* and he did it to impress Jodie Foster" (*Fox News*, April 30, 2007). The violent award-winning movie was directed by Martin Scorsese.

When *Natural Born Killers* was released in 1994 it inspired a young couple from Oklahoma to set out on what they planned to be a killing spree that left one person dead

---

1 http://www.leonardo-dicaprio.com/rec-new.html

2 http://www.bilkent.edu.tr/~jast/Number11/Amador.htm

3 http://digitaljournalist.org/issue0108/apocalypse.htm

and another paralyzed from the neck down. Seven years after their crimes, through numerous court hearings and appeals, the First Amendment rights of the defendants were upheld, but at a heavy price.

Despite a preponderance of evidence that young people are influenced to commit violent crimes by what they see in the media, and despite numerous instances of "copycat crimes," the media was basically absolved of blame for the actions of these perpetrators. A dozen deaths and other violent incidents on two continents were linked directly or indirectly to *Natural Born Killers*, yet the media continue to depict violence in such a way as to glorify it.[4]

Faith In Idols

Fans shape their bodies and souls to be like those they love. They want to talk like them, dress like them, look like them, and some will even kill like them. The little girl who imitates the way Britney Spears looks, dresses, and sings really does think Britney is her on-screen image. She and millions of others don't separate the image from the real person. It's a mystery to them when their idol divorces her husband, puts herself into a treatment center, and shaves her head.

An actor can even have a mesmerizing influence over much of their adoring public.[5] The fans have *faith* in their idol and they believe what their idol says—whether negative or untrue—about God, Jesus Christ, and the Bible. If the actor

---

4 (See www.crimelibrary.com/notorious_murders/celebrity/natural_born_killers/1.html).

5 "Studies conducted in Oak Park, Mich., in 1977 and followed up in 1992 showed that "women who watched violent television shows as children in the 1970s are more physically aggressive and more capable of committing criminal acts today." The women who scored at the top of categories "watched aggressive female heroines in the media as children and continued to do so as adults." These results "confirmed some of our worst fears," indicates L. Rowell Huesman, a psychology professor and researcher in the Aggression Research Group at the University of Michigan Institute for Social Research, Ann Arbor." *USA Today*, Jan. 1998 by Joe McNamara.

says that he protects his kids from the Bible or that he hates God, they don't separate the idol from the actor.

Look at these few examples (among many) of Hollywood's disdain for the God of the Bible. In *The Mosquito Coast*[6] staring Harrison Ford and River Phoenix, a weirdo calling people "brother" passes Harrison Ford and gives some kids a Bible, and says, "There you are. I've got a gift for you. It's the latest—*The Blue Jeans Bible*." Harrison Ford takes it and says, "Look at this, kids. It's just what I've been warning you about."[7]

In *Dogma,*[8] a comedy staring Ben Affleck and Matt Damon, the comedy gets a little serious when Matt Damon says:

> Now the carpenter, which is an obvious reference to Jesus Christ, who was raised a carpenter's son, he represents the Western religions … Organized religion destroys who we are by inhibiting our actions … by inhibiting our decisions, out of, out of fear of some, some intangible parent figure who, who shakes a finger at us from thousands of years ago and says, and says, "Do it—Do it and I'll f------' spank you.[9]

Robin Williams in *Patch Adams* looks to the heavens and says:

> You created man. Man suffers enormous amounts of pain. Man dies. Maybe you should have had a few more brain-storming sessions prior to creation. You rested on the seventh day. Maybe you should've spent that day on compassion. You know what? You are not worth it.

---

6 Nominated for 2 Golden Globes.

7 http://www.script-o-rama.com/movie_scripts/m/mosquito-coast-script-transcript-ford.html

8 Six nominations, including "Independent Spirit Award."

9 http://www.imdb.com/title/tt0120655/

In *The Simpsons*[10], one of the kids is asked to thank God for a meal. He says, "Dear God. We paid for all this stuff ourselves, so thanks for nothing."

During another episode in a bowling alley, Homer Simpson's decapitated head rolls slowly down the lane toward pins impaled with spikes, driving one of them into the skull, which pops open to reveal a note: "I owe you one brain. Signed, God." Lisa Simpson mockingly describes prayer as "the last refuge of the scoundrel."[11]

Hollywood is fostering a growing hostility towards Christians and influencing an entire generation. See if you can spot the common thread running through modern movies:

• George Clooney[12] asks a man in a cheap suit (with a large patch over one eye), "What kind of work do you do?" The man enthusiastically answers, "Sales, Mr. McGill, sales! And what do I sell? The truth, every blessed word of it—Genesis right on down to Revelation. That's right, the Word of God. Let me tell you there is d-mn good money in, in times of woe and want."

• A man in a cheap black suit, wearing large-brimmed black hat, with really weird eyes (holding a large wooden cross in one hand, with another large cross pinned to his suit) stands on a New York sidewalk and says, "The good Lord still loves me. He loves all of His children. Why He loves you ... Help ma! He's burning me alive. He's burning me!"

---

10 *The Simpsons* is an Emmy and Peabody Award-winning American animated sitcom created by Matt Groening for the Fox Network. *Thank God It's Doomsday* typifies the screen-writer's message. God is the almighty ruler of the Universe. He once attempted to flood Springfield (the Simpson's home town), but was stopped when Reverend Lovejoy showed that God was the path to good, and also once chose to end the world. This time, he was stopped by Homer Simpson, who requested him to turn back time and leave the apocalypse off for a few years. God has two aides, Colonel Sanders and Buddha, although he is seen with Jesus in Heaven.

11 "Anything goes: moral bankruptcy of television and Hollywood," *USA Today*, Jan. 1998 by Joe McNamara.

12 For George Clooney's beliefs, see *What Hollywood Believes* by Ray Comfort.

• A devious-looking weirdo dressed in white, with long blond hair and a large cross around his neck is preaching on a sidewalk. A sane-looking and mystified Jodie Foster slowly walks by and looks at them as they chant a slow and horrible-sounding "Praise God, praise the Lord, praise God." Like a salivating wolf, the weirdo then drips with lust as he looks at her. He later on in the movie blows himself up (murdering many others), to prove his commitment against the progress of science. He showed that he was prepared to die to stop anything that might prove there is no God. The movie is strongly pro-evolution, and it's message is that Christianity is for simpletons and murderous weirdos.

Michael Medved, film critic and author of *Hollywood vs. America,* said:

But the attitude you have from Hollywood, where every time someone in today's world is portrayed as some kind of religious believer, that person is viewed as some kind of a crook, or deviant, or weirdo, or an ugly person, or something is wrong with him or her, it's poisonous.[13]

Worth a Thousand Words

A picture is worth a thousand words, so let's look at one picture, particularly its script. This is edited from an award-winning R-rated movie called *Blow*, directed by Ted Demme. It is the story of George Jung, the man who established the American cocaine market in the 1970s. As you read it, ask yourself why Mohamed, Buddha or the Dalai Lama didn't make it into the script. Why only Jesus? And why use His name in conversation anyway? Johnny Depp is "George" and Penelope Cruz is "Mirtha." Note: Three times the "f" word was used in conjunction with the name of Jesus:

TUNA: "Jesus Christ."
GEORGE: "Jesus Christ. Jesus ------- Christ."

MR. T (cont'd.): "Jesus Christ."

MR. T (cont'd.): "Jesus, ---- me running!"

DIEGO: "Jesus Christ, George, I don't see you in two years ..."

GEORGE: "Jesus Christ."

GEORGE: "Jesus ------- Christ, Diego."

MIRTHA: "Oh, Jesus Christ, George."

DR. BAY: "Oh, Jesus, Get me a 12-lead."

DEREK: "Jesus, is that Mirtha!?"

LEON: "Jesus, George, fifteen percent. That's an extra two-hundred large."[14]

The director, Ted Demme, died less than a year later after the movie's release, while playing basketball. Cocaine was found in his system.[15]

Wheel of Fortune's host, Pat Sajak[16] has been working in Hollywood for more than thirty years. He said:

To quote Mr. [Rob] Reiner[17], "Movies are basically advertising cigarettes to kids." No knock on Rob. In fact, I agree with him. But why is smoking open to censorship and not these other issues? And what happened to Hollywood's argument that movies and TV shows don't *cause* bad behavior, they just reflect it? ...The answer is, there is no answer. It's just Hollywood being Hollywood. *It's monumental hypocrisy.* Kids can't pick up bad habits from what they watch ... oh, except for smoking.

---

14 http://sfy.ru/sfy.html?script=blow

15 http://imdb.com/title/tt0221027/

16 Host of *Wheel of Fortune*, television production company owner, radio station owner (Annapolis, MD), music publisher, board member of the American Cinema Foundation

17 As the son of multi-talented comedic genius Carl Reiner (*Your Show of Shows*), Rob Reiner instantly outgrew his father's legacy to establish himself as an independent force in multiple facets of the entertainment industry.

Directed By Hollywood

In speaking of the mass killing of 32 people on April 16, 2007, at Virginia Polytechnic Institute and State University, a Fox News commentator said that in his manifesto, mass murderer Cho Seung-hui was "railing against Christianity." NBC news said the same thing—that his manifesto was full of violence, profanity and "railed against Christianity." Why wasn't he railing against Islam or some other religion? Other commentators used phrases such as "just like in the movies" to describe how he took the lives of his fellow students. They also revealed that Cho Seung-hui's heroes were Columbine killers Eric Harris and Dylan Klebold. In reference to evolution and their planned killing spree, Harris had written, "You know what I love? Natural Selection! It's the best thing that ever happened to the Earth. Getting rid of all the stupid and weak organisms." He added "Sometime in April me and [Klebold] will get revenge and will kick natural selection up a few notches."[18]

Here are two more transcripts. They weren't written directly by Hollywood. They are from two young amateur filmmakers—Eric Harris and Dylan Klebold, made prior to the assault on Columbine High School, assembled from the Columbine Report and *Time* Magazine.[19] Note: Four times the "f" word when referring to these Christians and to Jesus:

> Dylan: "I don't like you, Rachel and Jen [two of their victims], you're stuck up little b------, you're ------- little… Christians. Godly little whores!"[20]

---

18 www.msnbc.msn.com/id/12370508

19 http://www.time.com/time/magazine/article/0,9171,1101991220-35870,00.html

20 If the world hates you, you know that it hated me before it hated you. If you were of the world, the world would love his own: but because you are not of the world, but I have chosen you out of the world, therefore the world hates you. Remember the word that I said to you, The servant is not greater than his lord. If they have persecuted me, they will also persecute you; if they have kept my saying, they will keep yours also. But all these

Eric: "Yeah … 'I love Jesus! I love Jesus!' Shut the f--- up!"

Dylan: "What would Jesus do? What the f--- would I do?" (He acts like he's shooting the camera with his hand, with sound to accompany it.)

Eric: "I would shoot you in the mother-------- head! Go Romans! Thank God they crucified that -------."

Eric and Dylan: "Go Romans!" "Go Romans!!" "Yeah!!" "Wooo!"

On April 20th, 1999, 30 minutes before the attack (Evidence item #200):

Eric: "Say it now."

Dylan: "Hey mom. I gotta go. It's about a half an hour till judgment day. I just wanted to apologize to you guys for any c--- this might instigate as far as (inaudible) or something. Just know I'm going to a better place. I didn't like life too much, and I know I'll be happy wherever the ---- I go. So I'm gone. Good-bye. Reb …"[21]

The only difference between the Columbine killings and Leonardo DiCaprio's on screen killings was that the two murderers targeted only Christians. I wonder why.

---

things will they do to you for my name's sake, because they know not him that sent me." (John 15:18-21)

21 http://www.acolumbinesite.com/quotes.html

You Shall Commit Adultery

How far Hollywood has come since the days when it offered free land to anyone who built a church in the area. It has become a modern day Sodom. It is an evil that has been responsible for destroying this country's moral foundations. It is responsible for promoting alcohol, tobacco[1] and illicit drugs, for mocking the gospel[2], aggressively promoting the homosexual agenda, promoting unspeakable

---

1 Hollywood Stars Encourage Youngsters to Smoke, www.mascotcoalition.org

2 On December 11, 2006, actor Charlie Sheen gave a "vulgar adaptation," as the American Family Association described it, of a few favorite Christian Christmas carols, including "Joy to the World." The Monday episode of *The Late Show* opened with Sheen singing about his sexual activity to the Christmas tunes. "CBS approved Sheen's adaptation of the favorite Christmas carol, making it into a vulgar sex song," said Donald E. Wildmon, Chairman of AFA, in a statement. "The network and sponsors paid Sheen to mock Christ, Christmas and Christians. Many in the Christian community are growing tired of this bigotry by the networks and Hollywood." www.christianpost.com

Early March 2007, Comedy Central rebroadcasted an episode of the *Sarah Silverman Program* on Thursday in which the female comedian has sex with "God." The installment, titled "Batteries," first aired Wednesday night and features a "one-night-stand" with a "Black God," whom Sarah Silverman tries to brush-off the morning after. Many Christians disagree strongly with the rebroadcast, noting that the content is extremely insensitive and degrading toward religion. One such group, the Timothy Plan, has urged Christians to boycott the network's parent company, Viacom, and pull out from all investments with them. www.christianpost.com

violence[3], adultery, rape, blasphemy, lying, greed, and every evil possible.[4]

Hollywood has set its own standard and become a law to itself. It answers to no-one and rules as the only potentate. It says, Thou shalt commit adultery, lie, steal, kill, blaspheme and covet. Its first and greatest commandment is Thou shalt have any other gods before the God of the Bible.

Jody Eldred is an Emmy-Award-winning producer-director. He said:

> "Did you know that nine out of ten Hollywood films lose money? Did you know that the vast majority of new television shows are cancelled because no one is watching them? Do you wonder why?" The obvious answer, says Eldred, is "because they're mostly awful." But *why* are they awful? "Because," notes Eldred, "the people creating them are completely out of touch with the people they are creating them for! Their worldview is vastly different from the worldview of most Americans. We have a largely Christian nation, but Hollywood is largely un-Christian, and in many if not most cases, anti-Christian. They're not just out of touch. They're against you!"[5]

Biblical Christianity is anathema in Hollywood because those who truly love the God of Scripture will no longer show up at the box office to pay for movies that glorify that which is

---

3 If viewers aren't influenced by what they see and hear why then do advertisers pay $2.6 million to air 30 second advertisements during the Super Bowl? *Billions* of dollars are spent each year and advertisers get their returns of their dollars *because* viewers are influenced.

4 "Over the past 40 years, Hollywood has been primarily responsible for the rapid degeneration of our culture. Modern cinema is filled with violence, sadism, sex at its most animalistic, crudeness, nihilism and despair. If Hollywood wants to treat Christianity as the antithesis of all it holds dear, Christians should feel complimented." Why Hollywood Hates Christianity, www.frontpagemag.com

5 "Why Hollywood is Insane," www.worldnetdaily.com/news/article.asp?ARTICLE_ID=52626

abhorrent to Him. Hollywood's income is built on the things that it loves—lawlessness, adultery, lust, fornication, violence and greed, and as long as this world is kept from turning to God, it will continue to pay Hollywood its dues.

If an actor becomes involved in Scientology, Kabala, Buddhism, atheism or any strange religion, he or she will have Hollywood's blessing. However, if he or she is genuinely converted to Jesus Christ, they have sinned in Hollywood's eyes, and his or her career may face the death sentence.

What Should You Do?

So, how can *you* make a difference? How can one person influence the powerful Goliath of the entertainment industry? The answer is in your own hands. You have a powerful sling that can hit the blaspheming giant right between the eyes, and believe me, it will leave a deep impression on his mind.

Make it your aim to never pay Hollywood to see sex and blasphemy. Every time we give any money to see any motion picture we are lining the pockets of the producers. We are saying, "Good work. Love it! Keep them coming!" That's the message we send if it's a good clean movie, and it's the message we send if it's a filthy, dirty movie.

A few years ago, there was a movie called *The Time Changer*.[6] It was about a Christian gentleman from a hundred or so years ago, who invented a time machine that brought him into the era of modern Christianity. He joined a contemporary church and found himself doing things the rest of the congregation did—he found himself watching a modern movie. But shortly after he entered the theater, he ran out into the lobby with a look of pain on his face, crying, "They blasphemed the name of the Lord! There must be a mistake! *They blasphemed[7] His name.* Stop this!"

---

6 You can get *The Time Changer* at www.christianfilms.com

7 Even in the United States there are some states that still officially have blasphemy laws on the books. Massachusetts, for example, still has a law under Chapter 272 of its general laws; Section 36: "Whoever willfully

Many years ago, I went with my daughter (when she was fourteen years old) to see a movie that had been enthusiastically recommended by a Christian. Within five minutes of the beginning, the name of Jesus was blasphemed, so we immediately walked out.

What good did that do? We had already paid for the tickets. We walked out because I want to set an example for my daughter. If I sit through a movie that blasphemes the name of Jesus, I'm saying "It's okay" to Hollywood, and I'm saying to her, "you can do what I'm doing." You can worship Jesus on Sunday and sit through a movie that uses His name in place of a word used to describe human waste. That's hypocrisy, and I would rather lose my right arm than have my daughter think that I'm a hypocrite. That's my standard. Yours may be higher.

You say, "But if I had that standard I would rarely get to see a modern movie!" That may be true, and it shows how far America has fallen. But being a Christian means taking up the cross and denying yourself. It means denying myself the pleasure of entertainment, denying Hollywood income, and most importantly, honoring God.

So, what's the big deal with using God's name in vain? Movies simply reflect culture, and that's how people talk nowadays—it's just a word. Not to God. Using God's name in vain is more serious than a heart attack. The Old Testament gives the death sentence for blasphemy, and that same Law will be enforced on the Day of Judgment.[8] The Lord will not hold him guiltless who uses His name in vain.[9]

---

blasphemes the holy name of God by denying, cursing or contumeliously reproaching God, his creation, government or final judging of the world, or by cursing or contumeliously reproaching Jesus Christ or the Holy Ghost, or by cursing or contumeliously reproaching or exposing to contempt and ridicule, the holy word of God contained in the holy scriptures shall be punished by imprisonment in jail for not more than one year or by a fine of not more than three hundred dollars, and may also be bound to good behavior."

8 See Romans 2:12.

9 Exodus 20:7: You shall not take the name of the LORD your God in vain; for the LORD will not hold him guiltless that takes his name in vain.

Look at this news release from early in 2007:

ATLANTA (AP) — So much for God and country, at least during some in-flight showings of the Oscar-nominated movie *The Queen.* All mentions of God are bleeped out of a version of the film distributed to Delta and some other airlines.

Jeff Klein, president of Jaguar Distribution, the Studio City, Calif., company that supplied the movie to the airlines earlier this month, said it was a mistake, committed by an overzealous and inexperienced employee who had been told to edit out all profanities and blasphemies.

"A reference to God is not taboo in any culture that I know of," Klein said. "We excise foul language, excessive violence and nudity."

Airline passengers watching the movie hear "(Bleep) bless you, ma'am," as one character speaks to the queen. In all, the word "God" is bleeped seven times. (At no time in the original movie is "God save the queen" uttered.)

Klein said he discovered the mistake after a London-bound Air New Zealand passenger complained. Jaguar has been sending out new, unedited copies to the airlines. Airlines routinely show movies from which graphic scenes and strong profanities are edited out.

The "overzealous and inexperienced employee" had been told to remove filthy offensive words from the movie. So he removed the name of God. What does that say about him, and what does it say about Hollywood?

Hallowed Be Thy Name

God's name is to be revered. It is to be honored. It is to be *hallowed*. But Hollywood doesn't do that. It does the opposite. It takes it in *vain*. The definition of something that is taken in "vain" means that it is considered "worthless, empty, or hollow."

If I went to a movie and for some reason the producer decided to have an actor say that my wife was a prostitute, I would immediately leave the theater. I don't care how much I am enjoying the movie, *I would not sit back and let anyone insult the good name of my precious wife.*

Now let's bring it closer to the issue. Imagine if, for some strange reason, the actor began to equate my wife's name with a filthy cuss word? What a terrible insult it would be to her character if I was even *tempted* to sit there for a second, because I liked the movie! If I did so, you would be justified in questioning my love for her.

How much more should I be jealous of the good name of the God who gave me my wife and gave me life itself? How much more should I esteem the name of the One who suffered and died on the cross for me?

If a Hollywood producer for some reason decides to put the "f" word before the name "Jesus Christ," I don't care how entertaining the movie is, I will not pay to listen to that, no matter how good the story line.

Godly Jews won't *speak* or even *write* the Name of G-d because they consider it so holy.[10] Yet we *pay* Hollywood actors to use it in blasphemy for our entertainment and pleasure.

Christianity Today cited a study that looked at the movie-viewing habits of "religious" Americans. They found that when it came to watching R-rated films, "there isn't much difference between the religious and nonreligious."[11]

---

10 Jews interpret the law given by Moses as a prohibition against transcribing the name of God, because they feel that if God is recorded onto a piece of paper, there is the possibility that the name will be disrespected or destroyed in some way. The general concern with writing G-d in its true form is that it might be erased, defaced by being crossed out or scribbled upon, torn, thrown in the trash, or ravaged in some other way. Writing G-d instead of God communicates the writer's idea effectively, but since G-d is incomplete, there is no risk of defacement. http://www.wisegeek.com/why-do-jews-write-g-d-instead-of-god.htm

11 http://www.christianitytoday.com/movies/commentaries/rratedmovies.html

Home Delivery

With the advent of cable TV, now anyone can have R-rated movies pumped into their home. No longer is there the concern about someone from church or the workplace seeing you at a dirty movie. What's more, these movies have no moral boundaries—"This kind of programming—a mix of violence, sex and sophomoric stunts—is bursting out all over basic cable, which is not regulated by the Federal Trade Commission and is therefore, theoretically, reined in only by concerns of cable operators and advertisers."[12]

Every Christian has his own liberty before God, but I'm curious to know how do they react when they hear blasphemy?[13] Do they blush, not notice it, or just whisper a sincere apology to the Lord? (Check out video clips at www.hollywoodandgod.com.)

An actor friend of mine once called me and said that he had been offered a great movie deal, but he had a problem with one part of the script. The story line was wonderful, but as usual in a romantic movie, it included an intimate conversation and ended with a passionate kiss. He would get $100,000 for doing the movie, but he said, "I won't kiss another woman like that, and besides, what would my kids think of me if they saw the movie?" He turned down the part because it could also be used to undermine his Christian testimony.

I greatly respected him for it. Think of it. Could you bring yourself to kiss someone other than your spouse for ten seconds—for $100,000?

The incident reminded me of a story I heard of an English Prime Minster who during a dinner leaned over to the woman sitting next to him, and said, "Would you go to bed with me for a million dollars?" She said, "I would think about it." He then asked, "Would you go to bed with me for one dollar?" She widened her eyes and said, "What kind of woman do you

---

12 http://www.ucg.org/commentary/moralmind.htm

13 "Wherefore I give you to understand, that no man speaking by the Spirit of God calls Jesus accursed..." (1 Corinthians 12:3).

think I am!" He replied, "Madame, we have already established that. Now we are just negotiating the price."

For what price should a Christian prostitute himself? What amount tempts us to compromise our convictions? $100,000? One dollar? An entertaining movie? God isn't impressed with the cost, and neither should we be impressed with anything the world offers us. We are called to live out our convictions, not to be hypocrites.

Peeping Tom

Imagine your indignation if you found a peeping Tom peeping through your bedroom window at night. You would probably call the police and have the dirty pervert arrested. But if you have ever found pleasure by watching a sexually explicit scene in a movie, you are a peeping Tom—a lust-filled, heavy breathing pervert. The only difference is that you pay a fee to peep through a window you call a movie screen. Remember that God says that if you even *look* with lust you are committing adultery in the heart.[14]

So, if you and I are going to support Hollywood's film industry, here's our biblical Movie Guide:

"Whatsoever things are true, whatsoever things are honest, whatsoever things are just, whatsoever things are pure, whatsoever things are lovely, whatsoever things are of good report; if there be any virtue, and if there be any praise, think on these things" (Philippians 4:8).

"I will set no wicked thing before mine eyes …" (Psalm 101:3).

Why are so many who profess to be Christians feeding on R-rated movies that are filled with violence, filthy language,

---

14 "You have heard that it was said by them of old time, You shall not commit adultery: But I say to you, That whosoever looks on a woman to lust after her has committed adultery with her already in his heart" (Matthew 5:27-28).

blasphemy, and graphic sex scenes? Perhaps it's because magazines like *Christianity Today*[15] (despite Philippians 4:8 and Psalm 101:3) actually promote them:

> *The Number 23* is rated R for violence, disturbing images, sexuality and language. The Lord's name is taken in vain along with all the big swear words. There's very graphic, bloody and sudden violence—throats being slit and bodies dropping on pavement. There's no nudity, but there are several sex scenes that show a lot of action—and degrees of perversion such as violent sex[16].

The magazine kindly provides a "Talk About It—Discussion Starters" section—for after you have peeped at the "lot of action" sex and listened to them blaspheme the Lord's name.

Hollywood producer Ralph Winter says, "I've made R-rated movies, and if I think that's warranted, I'll do it again, because sometimes you need to show the depravity of where people come from, to show how they can be changed into something else."[17]

> "Ralph is important to the Christian community of Hollywood, because he is a living breathing witness of what it takes for Christians to acquire power and influence here. [He's] a wonderful combination of professionalism and integrity, and godliness. He has made it to the highest level in Hollywood, without losing his faith in Jesus, and without

---

15 *Christianity Today* is an Evangelical Christian periodical based in Carol Stream, Illinois. It is the flagship publication of its parent company Christianity Today International, claiming circulation figures of 150,000 and readership of 350,000. It was started in 1956 as counter-point to *The Christian Century* (the predominant independent periodical of mainline Protestantism) and as a way to bring the evangelical Christian community together, the magazine was founded by Billy Graham.

16 http://www.christianitytoday.com/movies/reviews/2007/number23.html

17 http://www.cbn.com/cbnnews/news/

the kind of nauseating rationalizations that many Christians eventually make to achieve success here."[18]

Winter calls himself a Christian and yet sees fit to produce films that blaspheme the name of God and the name of Jesus.[19]

> And Winter says that Christians better beware of hypocrisy when they judge their Hollywood brothers for making R-rated entertainment, because … believers must be going to a lot of those questionable movies, or those films would not make so much money.[20]

It's Not Okay

It's become popular for church websites to give a little insight into the pastor's likes and dislikes, so that you can get to know him better and perhaps imitate him. On one site, when the senior pastor is asked about his favorite movie, he says, "Tough one; I'm a movie freak—used to be *Lost Boys* (vampire movie)…I like anything intense, brutal, mind-bending, etc." His associate one-ups him. He answers, "*Snatch* with Brad Pitt and Benicio Del Toro. Great film if you can get past the 493 F-bombs!" Apparently he got past them without a problem. Actually, he was exaggerating a little when he said that the movie used the "F" word 493 times. I located the original script and counted each time the word was used.[21] It was used 156 times, and the name of Jesus was blasphemed eleven times.[22]

Every dollar bill that is given to the box office goes towards helping to feed the giant. But when we don't pay

18 http://lookingcloser.org/ralphwinter-interview.htm

19 http://www.script-o-rama.com/movie_scripts/f/fantastic-four-script-transcript-alba.html

20 Ibid

21 http://www.bridgewaychristian.org

22 http://www.dailyscript.com/scripts/snatch.pdf

them to produce movies that blaspheme the name of God, we are saying to the producer and the script writers, "It's *not* okay."[23]

Protesting with the wallet gets the attention of the entertainment industry, because it articulates the only language Hollywood speaks. Mammon is their god:

> The studios learned an important lesson from Universal's Walden-financed Oscar-winning biopic, *Ray*, which was previewed at churches. Congregations loved the film but objected to the word "God" being used as a cuss. *Ray's* director, Taylor Hackford, who had already cut four-letter profanities to satisfy Anschutz, the Walden boss, insisted he would not edit the film further, but it cost Universal the support of some church advocates. As Hackford says: "People in Hollywood aren't stupid. It flies in the face of what I believe, but you're still working in the movie industry, not the movie art form."[24]

Hollywood's love of blasphemy only cost them "the support of some church advocates." But the Southern Baptist Convention, the nation's largest Protestant denomination, for eight years had a policy of not going to any movie Disney produced because of its support of homosexual-themed events and movie subjects. Although Disney never indicated that their bottom line had been effected, look at what happened back in July 2006:

> Famed family-film maker Disney is headed back to its roots, with confirmation yesterday of cuts of 650 employees that will include a phase-out of its R-rated movies.[25]

---

23 If you don't go to modern movies, you may like to consider passing this book onto someone whom you suspect does.

24 http://www.newstatesman.com/200511210029

25 http://worldnetdaily.com/news/article.asp?ARTICLE_ID=51167

It seems that Disney had already been feeling the pinch. A year or so earlier they took the drastic step of actually removing blasphemy from a script:

> Peter Sarsgaard,[26] co-star of the Jodie Foster Disney thriller *Flightplan*, had the exclamation "Jesus" removed from his lines of dialogue. "They said, 'You can't say that. You can't take the Lord's name in vain.' I had to say 'shoot', and that isn't as good."[27]

Perhaps Mr. Sarsgaard should have used his mother's name in place of human excrement. That might have been as good. Or if he wants to draw attention to the movie and himself, why doesn't he consider using the exclamation "Muhammed!"? It may be a first for Hollywood, and would probably get him some free publicity.

So, why don't we see actors blaspheming the name of Mohamed? There are probably two main reasons:

> 1. Screenwriters are aware that if they even draw a simple *cartoon* of Muhammed they could lose their head.[28]

> 2. Muhammed's name isn't despised enough to use as a cuss word. That's reserved for the Savior. He said that the

---

26 http://www.imdb.com/name/nm0765597/

27 Ibid

28 The *Jyllands-Posten* Muhammad cartoons controversy began after twelve editorial cartoons, most of which depicted the Islamic prophet Muhammad, were published in the Danish newspaper *Jyllands-Posten* on 9-30-2005. The newspaper announced that this publication was an attempt to contribute to the debate regarding criticism of Islam and self-censorship. In response, Danish Muslim organizations held public protests and spread knowledge of *Jyllands-Posten*'s publication thereby igniting the controversy. As it grew, examples of the cartoons were reprinted in newspapers in more than fifty other countries, which led to numerous death threats, attempted murder, bounties placed upon the heads of the cartoonists by Islamic leaders and numerous protests both peaceful and violent with some including rioting particularly in the Muslim world.

world would hate Him, because He would testify of their deeds—that they are evil.[29]

Hollywood's Redeeming Features

Perhaps you are consoling yourself with the thought that contemporary Hollywood has been bad, but it does have some redeeming qualities. In recent years it has gained some merit points in the eyes of Christians because it has produced good movies such as C.S. Lewis's *The Chronicles of Narnia: The Lion, the Witch and the Wardrobe.* It *was* a great movie, but it had no clear gospel message. Only those with a keen eye for allegory would have found something.

Then there was the much awaited trilogy of *Lord of the Rings*. I sat through more than nine long hours, waiting for some sort of gospel message. There wasn't one. Not even in the faintest of allegories.

Facing the Giants was a good Christian movie. However, it wasn't a Hollywood production. It was produced by a church and the cast were church members.[30] The *Left Behind* movies were made by a Canadian company in Canada, with a Hollywood crew and cast.

The Passion of the Christ was not a Hollywood production. It was filmed in Europe. Mel Gibson financed it with his own money, and Hollywood hated it with a passion. They would be greatly offended if it was even slightly attributed to them.

---

29 "The world cannot hate you; but me it hates, because I testify of it, that the works thereof are evil." (John 7:7).

30 Produced by Sherwood Pictures, part of the media ministry of the Albany, Georgia-based Sherwood Baptist Church, the film was made on a limited budget with a cast and crew of volunteers. But *Giants* earned more than $4.4 million in three weeks of release. Playing at its widest point on 441 screens, the movie (www.christianmovies.com) centers on a losing high school football coach whose life turns around after he puts his faith in God. "What is unique about faith-based films is they don't accept traditional marketing approaches and don't trust Hollywood," Samuel Goldwyn president Meyer Gottlieb said. http://movies.ninemsn.com

Despite its incredible success (it grossed well over $700 million worldwide), it was virtually snubbed at the Oscars.[31]

Luther was a good movie, but again, it had no gospel message. Neither did Disney's production of *Prince of Egypt*, *The End of the Spear*, etc.

According to Gallup polls in recent years, 80 percent of Americans consider themselves Christian to some degree and 59 percent (177 million) attend religious services at least once a month. So it makes good business sense for Hollywood to pan for gold in the pews. However, Disney's 2007 effort to do so with *The Nativity Story* didn't yield any nuggets.[32]

The Problem

Here's the problem. Hollywood's moguls may give the Christian market movies that entertain, but they will certainly not make movies that promote what they consider to be "dangerous Christian fundamentalist propaganda"—what we call "the gospel." You have about as much hope of that happening as you have selling the Temple Mount to Jews for an Arab Israeli bacon burger drive-through.

So don't hold your breath for Hollywood to produce a movie that is going to present a clear gospel message.

---

31 "As a result, lots of us who love movies end up minimizing the obvious distortion in a project and focus on its subtle strengths. But the fact remains, if a good man would turn his face in disgust and shame from what is on the screen, that should inform our own discernment about a movie. We can get so caught up in technique that we are essentially gobbling down well-prepared sewage. 'Stunningly arranged!' 'Daringly conceived!' 'Strikingly performed!'—it's still just poisonous filth. What makes this year's nominations even darker is the fact that there was one big cinematic elephant that, as we all predicted, was passed over for all the top awards. This movie was … the biggest independent movie in cinema history … the third biggest box-office movie of the year … a movie that moved millions of people to tears, had the entire world talking, and even led several murderers to turn themselves in!" www.beliefnet.com/story/160/story_16008_1.html

32 It its opening weekend it grossed $7,849,304. Disney's production budget was $35 million. *The Passion of the Christ* grossed $83,848,082 on its opening weekend. Its production budget was $30 million. www.boxofficemojo.com/movies

If anything of that nature is produced, it will no doubt come *independently* from Christians within the industry. The only time Hollywood itself is really happy to hear the name of Jesus is in blasphemy.

Charlie Chaplin and Underage Girls

Even though free land was given to churches who located there, as soon as movies began around the year 1900, they contained sex and violence. Then, in 1921 there was public outcry when (among other things) a well-known actor was accused of rape and murder, a director was found murdered, and another actor died of a drug overdose. Hollywood was getting a bad image, so some studio heads hired a Presbyterian senator, William Hays[1], to try to clean up Hollywood and convince the nation that it wasn't all bad.

Hays persuaded the studios that abiding by a set moral standard was the safest and cheapest answer to their troubles. If the movie industry policed itself, government censorship wouldn't have to step in. Plus, the new "Hay's Code" was a big money-saving measure. Instead of paying to fix moral content after the film was done, the studios could simply follow the Code *before* making their movies, and everyone would be happy. So, it was adopted in 1930. It stated:

> Pointed profanity—this includes the words "God," "Lord," "Jesus," "Christ" (unless used reverently) "Hell," "S.O.B.," "damn," or every other profane or vulgar expression however used, is forbidden.

---

1 William Hays was a Presbyterian elder and Indiana politician. Axel Madsen. *Stanwyck*, HarperCollins: New York, NY (1994), page 93.

Then, in 1934, the code was *enforced*. It had the authority to review all movies and demand script changes. If a theater ran a film without the proper seal of approval it would be fined $25,000. The Code had successfully forced studios to toe the line. Consequently, Hollywood began producing those wonderful, award winning, heart-warming, family movies such as *Ben Hur: A Tale of Christ*,[2] *The Ten Commandments*, *It's a Wonderful Life*, and many others.

However, Hollywood knew that there was big money in sex and violence. So, during the 1950s, some found a way around the Hay's Code through the free speech clause of the First Amendment, and studios began to push the moral envelope.

In 1968 Hollywood officially abandoned the filmmakers' Code, and shifted the moral responsibility to the parents with what we now know as the Rating System.[3] The floodgates

---

2 The colorful 1959 version was the *most* expensive film ever made up to its time, and the most expensive film of the 50s decade. At $15 million and shot on a grand scale, it was a tremendous make-or-break risk for MGM Studios—and ultimately saved the studio from bankruptcy. It took six years to prepare for the film shoot, and over a half year of on-location work in Italy, with thousands of extras. It featured more crew and extras than any other film before it—15,000 extras alone for the chariot race sequence. It was one of the most honored, award-winning films of all time. *Titanic (1997)* and *The Lord of the Rings: The Return of the King (2003)* are the only films to tie this phenomenal record, although unlike this film, they came away *without* any acting Oscars. http://www.filmsite.org/benh.html

3 Jack Valenti, 85, [who] helped devise the "G" to "X" movie-rating system, died today at his home in Washington of complications from a stroke in March. As president of the Motion Picture Association of America from 1966 to 2004, Valenti ... helped create a voluntary rating system in 1968 that changed the way the studios classified a film's suitability for general audiences. This new arrangement was important because it kept government intrusion and citizen censors at bay, while allowing the artists' maximum freedom and the consumer to influence the marketplace by voting with his wallet.

were suddenly opened. That's when the serpent was let loose in the garden.

What Happened Is Anyone's Guess

For those who know nothing of the restraint that Hay's Code put on the entertainment industry, the change in movie morality is a mystery. America was like a quiet little town living in peace below a huge dam called Hollywood. In the 1950s the dam began to crack, and in 1968 it burst upon the town, flooding it and destroying its residents:

> America's mainstream entertainment industry has not always been so oblivious to the Christian market. Hollywood studios used to churn out biblical epics at a steady pace, raking in millions of dollars—and, sometimes, Oscars—with predictable crowd-pleasers. Cecil B. DeMille directed a number of biblical movies, including the silent screen classic *King of Kings* and the 1949 film *Samson and Delilah* with Hedy Lamarr and Victor Mature. Gregory Peck starred in *David and Bathsheba*, Anthony Quinn headed a star cast in *Barabbas*, Kirk Douglas starred in *Spartacus*, and a pre-political Charlton Heston brought down the house in both *The Ten Commandments* and *Ben-Hur*. And then, sometime in the 1960s, religiously-themed entertainment simply disappeared. Why that happened is anyone's guess; a hip disdain for traditional cultural mores, perhaps, or a heightened fear of offending religious minorities. In any event, it was a major, if underappreciated, break. For nearly 2,000 years, the story of Jesus and broader biblical epics had

---

The 1968 system—with its long-familiar ratings ranging from "G" for admittance of general audiences to "X" prohibiting those under 17—was credited with helping keep the American film market competitive with European companies. In Europe, filmmakers had long ventured into fare laden with adult language, nudity and other forms of explicitness that proved increasingly popular with changing tastes. (*Washington Post*, April 26, 2007).

infused the cultural environment of the average Westerner. Now those influences were suddenly nowhere to be seen.[4]

Why did young people become so openly sexually promiscuous in the 1960s? What influenced them to become rebellious around that time and cast off their parents' Judeo-Christian values? Why was it that the violent crime rate rose sharply in the late 1960s?[5]

> During the 1960s, decline and decay intensified in many cities. A series of urban riots put an exclamation point on a general feeling of disorder. Many streets and parks became threatening places. *Between 1963 and the early 1970s, the rate of violent crime more or less tripled in the United States.* By violent crime, I mean murder, manslaughter and robbery. So we had a tripling of the crime rate at a time when the country was, by and large, prosperous, in which the unemployment rate even among African-American adolescents was quite low[6] (italics added).

Good News for Gays

The end of the Hay's Code eventually translated into very good news for Hollywood's homosexual community:

> The demise of the Hays Code did not immediately translate into positive representations of homosexuals and bisexuals. Instead, what emerged were a few formulaic scenarios in which bisexual characters in film were presented ... Rumors of bisexuality have persisted about many performers, from James Dean to Cary Grant to Tom Cruise, but only a few actors such as Madonna, Joey Lauren Adams, Anne Heche, and Sandra Bernhard have openly revealed their bisexual identities. It is no coincidence that the majority of these actors are women, for female bisexuality

---

4 www.washingtonmonthly.com/features/2004/0406.sullivan.html#byline

5 http://en.wikipedia.org/wiki/Crime_in_the_United_States

6 http://www.pbs.org/fmc/segments/progseg13.htm

is still much more acceptable than male bisexuality, since it plays into a particular male heterosexual fantasy.

An especially interesting instance of bisexual infiltration is the Julia Roberts film *My Best Friend's Wedding* (1997), which opens with bisexual singer Ani DiFranco's tongue-in-cheek cover of Dusty Springfield's "Wishin' and Hopin'" played over the credits. The film also starred bisexual actor Rupert Everett, who stole the show as the predictably loveable, laughable gay sidekick to Roberts' lead.

Bisexuality in film, as separate from gay and lesbian representation, has emerged as a significant genre in its own right, even spawning a separate bisexual film festival in San Francisco.[7]

So nowadays it is morally acceptable in Hollywood for Leonardo DiCaprio (and other well-known "leading men") to passionately kiss another man on screen.[8]

Back in 2004, Hollywood released *Saved!* It was produced by homosexual-rights advocate Brian Dannelly. The production staff was mostly composed of homosexuals and homosexual advocates, who used the film to mock God and Jesus Christ and to demonize Christians, while glorifying the homosexual lifestyle.[9] In the movie Jesus appears to Mary in a vision and commands Mary to "save" Dean from homosexuality by having sex with him. Mary soon becomes angry at God and begins to doubt her Christian faith when she realizes that she is pregnant. During one scene in the film, Mary is staring at a cross and begins to spew vulgar profanity for the first time in her life. The story then continues as Dean's parents find his secret collection of homosexual pornography.

---

7 http://www.glbtq.com/arts/bisex_film,2.html

8 "I did get to play gay once, and I showed more than Colin Farrell shows in *Alexander*, though," he jokes, about his role in *Total Eclipse*. For any who are curious, there are more than a couple of scenes in *The Aviator* where DiCaprio is buck naked. "But it's PG-13, this time," he jokes. "You only get to see __ ___." Leonardo DiCaprio, www.wildaboutmovies.com/

9 http://bizpr.news.prweb.com/releases/2004/6/prweb132849.htm

Dean is then sent by his Christian parents to a homosexual rehabilitation center. At this center, Dean falls in love with another boy as they share the same room.

In addition, a wacky youth pastor and the principal of a Christian school prances around, making remarks, such as, "Are you ready to get your Jesus on?" This same youth pastor commits adultery with Mary's mother. In another scene, a girl speaks profanity in "pig Latin" as she intentionally exposes her body at a school assembly. The film climaxes at the Christian prom when Dean arrives with his homosexual lover and declares, "I know in my heart that Jesus still loves me!"

When asked about his own faith in God, the producer said:

> Faith is a journey. I'm always in conscious contact, even during a period when I didn't believe anything. You know what? I said I'm just not going to believe in anything. I'm going to start with personal responsibility and kindness. There's not going to be any reward system or punishment system. That's going to be my system. Not God.[10]

Hollywood Family

Hollywood's popular TV show "The Family Guy"[11] was said of www.tv.com to be "Sick, twisted, politically incorrect and freakin' sweet, the animated series features the adventures of the Griffin family. Peter and Lois have three kids—the

---

10 http://www.christianitytoday.com/movies/interviews/briandannelly.html

11 *Family Guy*'s first and second seasons were made starting in 1999 after Larry shorts (its predecessor) caught the attention of the Fox Broadcasting Company during the 1999 Super Bowl commercial. Its cancellation was announced, but then a shift in power at Fox and outcry from the fans led to a reversal of that decision and the making of a third season, after which it was cancelled again. Reruns on Teletoon (and later Adult Swim) drove interest in the show up, and the DVD releases did quite well, selling over 2.2 million copies in one year and renewing network interest. Family Guy returned to production in 2004, making two more seasons (for a total of five) and a straight to DVD movie, *Stewie Griffin: The Untold Story*. The sixth season is in production to air in the fall of 2007, with a seventh season airing in the fall of 2008.

youngest is a brilliant, sadistic baby bent on killing his mother and destroying the world." On one show Jesus of Nazareth is depicted as a teenager arguing with Joseph: "Up yours, Joseph! You're not my real dad!" Jesus phones Heaven, where God the Father answers while lying in bed with a woman. God hangs up on Jesus and leers at the woman ... God responds: "Oh, come on, baby. It's my birthday."

There are other examples of sexuality and mockery that are so sick I would rather not put them in print. Consider this study finding:

> Roughly six out of ten of the portrayals of religion on reality-based (unscripted television) shows were positive. That still doesn't reflect public opinion, but it's close. Unscripted shows were responsible for only 4.5 percent of the negative portrayals this study team found. The other 95.5 percent came from Hollywood's professionals, who are at their most comfortable attacking that which Christians hold dear. Television screenwriter Lloyd Billingsley pinpointed: "In the unwritten constitution of television ... God is effectively written out of existence and Judeo-Christian values on such things as adultery and divorce are disregarded."[12]

The Federal Communications Commission (the FCC) says that it's okay for Hollywood to do this, because it has created a "safe harbor":

> What is the "safe harbor"? The "safe harbor" refers to the time period between 10 p.m. and 6 a.m., local time. During this time period, a station may air indecent and/ or profane material. In contrast, there is no "safe harbor" for the broadcast of obscene material. Obscene material is entitled to no First Amendment protection, and may not be broadcast at any time. Are there certain words that are always unlawful? No. Offensive words may be profane

---

and/or indecent depending on the context. In the Golden Globe Awards Order, the FCC stated that it would address the legality of broadcast language on a case-by-case basis. Depending on the context presented, use of the "F-Word" or other words as highly offensive as the "F-Word" may be both indecent and profane, if aired between 6 a.m. and 10 p.m.[13]

In other words there is nothing to stop Hollywood from using filthy words along with the name of Jesus, if it is in the context of the story line, and if it is broadcast between 10 p.m. and 6 a.m.

But Hollywood has an aggressive agenda, and it has nothing to do with what its viewers want:

> According to an exclusive survey conducted by the Family Friendly Programming Forum, 80 percent of the U.S. adult population registered support for more family friendly TV programs during prime time, in a study of 1,000 representative households conducted by International Communications Research (ICR). While the desire for more family friendly programming hovers around 80 percent for most demographic segments—age, sex, household income, region, education and race—the support among parents with kids 6-17 years old is even higher. Nearly 90 percent of parents with kids 11-17, and nearly 86 percent of parents with kids 6-11, expressed a wish for more family friendly TV shows. (Source: Association of National Advertisers, Inc. Family Programming)[14]

Mickey Rooney[15] spoke of the vast chasm between Hollywood and the public when he denounced Hollywood's

---

13   http://www.fcc.gov/eb/oip/FAQ.html

14   http://www.dove.org/research/DoveFoundationROI-Study2005.pdf

15   Joe Yule Jr., also known as Mickey Rooney, was born September 23, 1920 in Brooklyn, New York. His parents, chorus girl Nell Carter and comic Joe Yule Sr., were vaudeville performers. Two weeks after Mickey's birth, he was on the road with the circuit traveling throughout North America.

insidious hatred for Christ as exemplified in *The Last Temptation of Christ.*[16] He said:

> "*The Last Temptation of Christ* provides a good example of the film establishment rallying around a bad film to protect its own selfish interest ... That film, no matter what its defenders say, was a slap to the face of Christians everywhere, but Hollywood cradled the picture as if it were *Citizen Cane.*"[17]

Jane Russell didn't pull any punches with her words:

At seventeen months old, his talent surfaced by accident. While hiding underneath a shoeshine stand in a Chicago theatre, fascinated by his father's act, he let out a sneeze. The noise caused a spotlight to find him in the crowd. Not knowing what to do he stood up and blew on his tiny toy mouth organ that was hanging on a string around his neck. The audience erupted with laughter. The show's manager got him a pint-sized tuxedo after the incident, and young Mickey began performing small ballads and speeches on stage. All in all, Mickey is a man with over 200 films under his belt. He earned an Honorary Oscar for Lifetime Achievement, a special Juvenile Oscar he shared with Deana Durbin in 1939, five Oscar nominations, one Emmy Award, five Emmy Nominations and two Golden Globes. http://www.mickeyrooney.com/biography.html

16 Martin Scorsese's *The Last Temptation of Christ* included a section in which Jesus Christ envisioned an ordinary life, including sex and marriage. "Aware of mounting organized pressure against the film, in 1987, Universal hires a liaison with the Christian community, a born-again Christian himself, and arranges a private advance screening for agitated groups, including Reverend Donald Wildmon's American Family Association and Bill Bright's Campus Crusade for Christ. The audience is especially disgusted by a closing image: Christ on the cross is tempted by Satan with visions of a "normal" life with the prostitute Mary Magdalene, replete with sex, marriage, and children. [In 1988] Edwards Theaters, with 150 theaters nationwide, refuses to screen the film, as do United Artists and General Cinemas, with 3,500 theaters between them. In August 1988, Universal opens *The Last Temptation of Christ* in nine major cities in the United States and Canada. The day before its premiere, Citizens for a Universal Appeal, a coalition of religious groups from Orange County, CA, stages a protest in front of Universal's L.A. headquarters that attracts some 25,000 participants." www.pbs.org/wgbh/cultureshock/flashpoints/theater/lasttemptation.html

17 http://www.goodfight.org/hwmission.html

"This Hollywood is not the place I was in. I wouldn't fit in these days with my beliefs. When people question me I just tell them I'm a mean-spirited, narrow-minded, conservative Christian bigot—not about race, but about those idiots trying to take the Ten Commandments off the wall, the Bible out of schools, and prayer even out of football games. I'm against kicking prayer and God out of the country. I don't like the ACLU and the liberal judges that threaten our religious freedoms. So label away!"[18]

Keep Our Money

In the early 1950s, America didn't have to lock its doors. It didn't have to lock its cars. A woman could walk on the sidewalks after dark without any real fear of getting raped, murdered, and dismembered. It was a time when you could pat a child on the head and not be concerned that you might look like a pedophile. It was a time when divorce was rare, when people were shocked by blasphemy, and when people went to church and were the real deal.

But for some reason, since the 1950s things have radically changed. What was once considered horrific has almost become accepted as the norm. God only knows how much of the blame lies at the feet of Hollywood for what they have done, simply to line their own pockets.[19] However, what concerns me more than anything else is that Hollywood has suppressed and mocked the gospel of everlasting life. The movie industry could have been used to promote so much good in this world, but it has pushed its evil agenda with a demonic zeal.

Please, don't fall into the trap of saying, "But I'm just one person. How could I influence Hollywood?" There are over 170 million people of faith in the United States. In 2005,

---

18 http://www.mediawisefamily.com/syw/i-russell.html

19 "70% of Americans say they are very or somewhat worried that popular culture, as depicted in television and movies, is lowering moral standards in the U.S. Hollywood takes much of the blame for this, as most say its products are driving down those moral standards." http://www.cbsnews.com/stories/2004/11/22/opinion/polls/main657068.shtml

roughly $.8.8 billion was spent on movie tickets in the U.S. According to The Barna Group, of that total, people of faith spent an estimated $6.94 billion. In other words, church-going people were responsible for *79% of the total domestic box office sales in 2005.* If we suddenly said, "Enough of the filth. We are no longer going to pay you for it," Hollywood would be forced to clean up its dirty act. And until that happens, the *billions* not spent lining the pockets of Hollywood each year could be instead channeled into helping the poor, or supporting missionaries, or into the local church.

So let's keep our money where our mouths are. If we say we have convictions as to what is right and what is wrong, we cannot play the hypocrite and support an industry that thrives on that which is abhorrent to the God we profess to love.

New York Jews

There was a human body lying on the floor of my bathroom in a New York hotel. We were in the Big Apple to shoot an episode for the third season of our television program. Seconds earlier I returned to my room on the fourteenth story, and was shocked to see that the door was cracked open. The body was that of a male in his 30s. There were no signs of a struggle, no blood, and no bruising on the neck area. It was something I would have expected in a dark alley, not in a high-rise in the heart of New York's Time Square.

Suddenly I heard a voice—"I've fixed the night-light under your sink. I'll be out of here in a minute."

"What's your name?" I answered.

"Harry."

"Harry, I have a question for you."

"Is it multiple choice?"

"Yes. What do you think happens after somebody dies? A. Heaven. B. Hell. C. Nothing."

Harry stood to his feet and said, "You go to sleep."

"You go to sleep? Are you a Jehovah's Witness?"

"Well, my mother is, and I lean in that direction."

Harry and I then spent about ten minutes talking together, as I reasoned with him about the injustice of the Jehovah Witness doctrine of "annihilation," and took him through the Ten Commandments. I gave him a "What Hollywood

Believes" CD, and as he left he told me that the talk had been helpful.

It was helpful for me also, because it gave me a little more confidence when speaking with a Jehovah's Witness. Meeting with Harry was ironic, because later that day we were filming a program on Jehovah's Witnesses and what they believed. The previous day a team of twelve of us had flown from Los Angeles to New York for filming. Stuart (Scotty) Scott sat next to me during the flight. Scotty loves salt. He even enlarged the holes in his personal salt shaker to get more of the tasty stuff faster. He embraces wholeheartedly the words of Jesus—"Salt is good."

During the flight, he looked at my laptop and boasted that his Pocket PC had a battery life that was twice mine. The PC was so small I cynically asked if it could do word processing. He explained that it could, but that it had to be written by hand on a screen, and then it miraculously translated the personal hand written words into a standard typeface. He picked it up and wrote, "My name is Scotty." We both then waited for a second or two and amazingly four typed words appeared on the screen. We almost had to rub our eyes in unbelief. They said, "My navel is Salty." So much for high tech. I decided to stay with my laptop.

God once and for all wrote His Word for humanity. He has made the way of salvation very clear, yet I almost have to rub my eyes in unbelief at the amazing way the Jehovah's Witnesses have interpreted that Word. They call themselves "Christians" but they blatantly deny the reality of Hell, the hope of Heaven for the believer, eternal punishment, the deity of Christ, the finished work of the cross, the necessity of the new birth, and the way of salvation.

They had already declined our request to their World Headquarters for an on-camera interview about what they believed, so we purchased a pair of high-tech digital video sunglasses and I snuck into their headquarters for interviews. During a one-hour period I was able to candidly talk to between fifteen and twenty Jehovah's Witnesses about their personal beliefs. We will of course make sure those interviewed keep their anonymity.

Jehovah's Witnesses not only shy away from cameras, but they officially refuse to take any literature, so it was strange for me to talk to people about the things of God and not leave them with any gospel tracts.

Earlier that day I stepped into an elevator in our hotel and passed out million dollar bill tracts to three people. One man was thrilled to get one. He immediately started reading it and said, "It's about God. It's religious. That's good." His loud mouth caused the lady next to me to say, "I don't want this. I will throw it in the trash." I kept my hands at my sides and said, "Please keep it. There's nothing more important than your eternal salvation."

Meanwhile, the man behind me was looking intently at the words written on the tract, and as he came to the Commandments he blurted out, "I've done all this. Seriously, I've done all this stuff!" His tone of voice revealed that he was deeply concerned. Mr. Loudmouth piped up, "That's okay. We all make mistakes." I wanted to say, "It's not okay," and they are not "mistakes." Suddenly the doors were open and we all parted company.

Jewish Heritage

Another one of our TV programs was to be on the subject of Judaism. Fortunately, Mark Spence, the Dean of our School of Biblical Evangelism, was able to secure an interview with the Rabbi of an orthodox New York synagogue. He informed me that anyone who was Jewish was allowed to take part in their service. Despite my mom being Jewish, I had never been to an orthodox synagogue, so I hooked up my spyglasses, put them on my forehead and walked into the meeting.

When I entered the premises I was instantly interrogated as to my Jewish heritage. What was my name? Was I Jewish? Was it on my mother or father's side? I said, "Mother." What was my mother's name? "Esther." Suddenly, I was wearing a Yuima and was part of the family of New York Jews, sitting among black-hats and curly side-burns, as they all nodded together. I was wearing shorts, wasn't dressed in black, I had trimmed sideburns and I wasn't nodding at all. I must have stood out like a California sore thumb.

About ten minutes into the proceedings, after the Torah had been placed in front of the Rabbi, he suddenly looked at me and said, "Ray, are you a Cohen? Is your family name 'Cohen?'

I called back, "I have an uncle called 'Cohen,'" and nodded as I answered.

It was the only nod I did during the entire service, but it sure had repercussions. It seemed the fact that my uncle was a Cohen was a big deal because the Rabbi quickly called me to the front, and before I knew what was happening, I was surrounded by helpful folk, was repeating a stack of Hebrew phrases, was picking up and putting down ribbons, and kissing the Torah.

This went on for five or ten minutes among much nodding and much to the excitement of those around me. I was a little dazed by the whole thing. I was then ushered to one side, and a thick book with Hebrew and English words was placed into my hands.

As I sat there thinking about what had just happened, I heard a whispered voice beside me say in a deep New York accent, "What an honor! What an honor! You are a 'Cohen.' That's amazing. You have been honored tonight. What an honor! A Cohen…"

I felt a little sick. I wasn't a Cohen. I was a "Comfort." I guess the Rabbi hadn't understood what I had said, and had taken my nod as a "Yes" and that meant I qualified for the priesthood. Oh dear.

Meanwhile, the whispering gentleman gave me a running commentary on the proceedings of the service. He explained to me why there was so much nodding going on among the singing, and the low mumbling, among other things. As he turned my page for me (I don't read Hebrew) he whispered,

"We are waiting for the Messiah."

"What are the signs of His coming?"

"There will be a trumpet sound."

"You mean the trumpet of the Archangel?"

"Yes, something like that. There have been many false Messiahs. Take Jesus. He was a Jew. We strung Him up. There were other false Messiahs that came after Him."

As the service drew to a close, our camera crew entered the room to set up the interview with the Rabbi. Meanwhile, I was being allowed to drink from a special glass filled with special grape juice.

It was after the drink that I noticed that I was surrounded by admirers. Ray Cohen, the cool dude in shorts with the hip sunglasses on his forehead was drinking the special juice from the special glass.

One of the admirers was a pale-faced, fourteen-year-old, sad-looking kid who was wearing what looked like his big brother's black hat. He was about to leave, so without much thought I decided to give him a million dollar bill tract. He would love it.

I said, "I have a gift for you. It's a million dollars."

The kid took it and stood there looking bewildered. It was as though I had handed him something that he wasn't supposed to have, and he didn't know what to do.

Suddenly, the bill was taken from his hand. Without a word, a gentleman began reading the message on the back. There was an intensity in the air. I felt as though I had just committed a serious crime and I had been caught red-handed. He quickly left with the damning evidence in his hand. Suddenly I heard the Rabbi call out in a very serious voice, "Ray. I want to talk to you outside, now!"

Outside, he held the undeniable proof of my sin in his hand, pointed to it and said, "What's with this J.C.! What is with this J.C.! I want everyone out now. They are to get out!"

I was no longer their pal. I was pleased that there were no stones around. "Hosanna" had turned into "Stone him!" in an instant. Wow. What a surprising difference Jesus makes.

We will look at why this happens, not only in Hollywood but in the rest of the Jewish community, in the next chapter.

Jesus, Hitler and Pedophiles

I'm always encouraged when I ask someone if they are a Christian and they answer "No. I'm Roman Catholic." It confirms something that most Catholics know but it seems that the world doesn't know. There is a difference between biblical Christianity and Roman Catholicism. Although the Roman church holds to some of the main tenants of the Christian faith, at its core it has its own entity. It has many highly-held traditions that are not found in the Bible. They are Roman Catholic traditions.

Consequently, it shouldn't surprise us that Jews are very difficult to reach with the gospel. This is because many of them equate Christianity with Roman Catholicism. And why shouldn't they? When they glance at the television news at Christmas or at Easter, who is upheld by the secular world as "the head of the Christian Church"? It's the pope.

Jews therefore believe that Christians bow down to graven images and they worship Mary and many other saints. To them, Christianity is a false religion, and one that should be kept at arm's length because at its very core it is in direct violation of the First and the Second of the Ten Commandments.

Many Jews even equate Christianity with Adolf Hitler. Central to his twisted philosophy was a belief in the inherent superiority of the German race. But *Christianity* doesn't preach superiority. It instead preaches that you are to love your neighbor as much as you love yourself. Jesus even said to love our *enemies*, to pray for those that despitefully use us, to turn the other cheek, to give to those that ask of us—to do good to *all* men. Biblical Christianity is soaked in love of humanity, while Hitler's philosophy was saturated in the blood of pure hatred. So it makes no sense that anyone in his right mind could confuse the two ... until we understand something important.

In pre-Second World War Germany, there were forty million Lutherans. It is significant to realize that to be part of the Lutheran church in those days one need not be converted to Christ. You were simply baptized into the church as a baby because you had to be a member to be married or buried. That was just the way it was. If you for some reason wanted to separate yourself from the church, your name would be read from the pulpit for three Sundays, and intercession was then made for you in public prayer. Consequently few took the radical step of leaving the church.

For years the denomination had been influenced by a theological liberalism that was really only secular philosophy disguised by religious language. So rather than being a vibrant Christ-centered lighthouse of biblical truth, the Lutheran church of that time (as with many contemporary denominations) was simply a huge traditional institution.[1]

After the First World War, Germany went into a massive recession. Adolf Hitler rose to political power by promising a return to dignity and prosperity for the German nation. He became their political "savior." Songs were sung in his honor—"Silent night! Holy night! All is calm, and all is bright. Adolf Hitler is Germany's wealth. Brings us greatness, favor and health. Oh give us Germans all power!"[2]

In 1932, Hitler appointed a man named Hermann Mueller to be head of the newly formed "German Christian Party." There was nothing "Christian" about this party. It was

---

1 *Day of No Return*, Kressmann Taylor (2003 edition. Originally published *Until That Day*, 1942) Xlibris, page 285.

2 http://www.j-cinstitute.org/Articles/Lyons_Idolatry.htm

merely a front for the Nazis to gain political strength through the massive Lutheran church. Hermann Mueller was then nominated as a candidate for the head of the church and vast amounts of money were spent on publicity.

The Nazis intimidated anyone who opposed their nominee, and when voting day came the only choice was: "Do you agree with the Fuehrer that Mueller must be Reichsbishop—Yes or No?" The Lutheran candidate wasn't even on the ballot.

With Mueller as head of the church the Nazis then had the power to appoint other leaders. Pastors who protested were either murdered and their churches closed, or they quietly disappeared into concentration camps. They were then replaced by Nazi "pastors," crosses at altars were replaced with pictures of Hitler, and Swastika flags were flown above their roofs.

These politically appointed pastors preached that any teaching about the existence of "sin" was false and created a complex of weakness in the German people. Biblical Christianity held them back from fulfilling their true destiny. They maintained that the German race was divine, and that God had chosen a new anointed leader—the blessed Hitler. He had been the savior that had been "lifted up" and "would draw all men to himself."[3] He would bring Germany into a new glory—a thousand year reign.

The pastors rejected the Old Testament, saying that it wasn't a Christian book—that its teachings had allowed the unclean and subtle doctrines of the Jew to dominate German thinking. No non-Aryan could hold any place of office in the church and anyone with Jewish roots must be purged from it. If someone had any Jewish ancestors he was encouraged to commit suicide. They said that it was a service to God to protect His worship from pollution—to join German with German and not to darken the nostrils of Heaven with the

---

3 *Day of No Return*, Kressmann Taylor (2003 edition. Originally published *Until That Day*, 1942) Xlibris, page 173.

sour, decaying breath of a Jew. The day had come "when the tares would be gathered and burned in the fire."

Replaced With *Mein Kampf*

But the Nazis soon found that pushing their politics from pulpits emptied church pews, so they began to meekly cloak their political agenda in biblical phraseology. Over time this left many of the more simple folk unable to distinguish the true pastor from the false.

On April 26, 1933, Hitler had said, "Secular schools can never be tolerated because such schools have no religious instruction, and a general moral instruction without religious foundation is built on air; consequently all character training and religion must be derived from faith ..."[4] But he later declared Nazism the state religion and the Bible was replaced by *Mein Kampf* in the schools. Throughout Germany he also removed pastors from their weekly hour of religious instruction in schools and replaced them with Nazi pastors, who subtly indoctrinated German youth with teachings about their superior "Aryan blood." They mocked the Bible and told them not to worship God but to worship the state and Adolf Hitler as its head. Their one aim was to destroy what they referred to as their "last enemy"—Christianity. Ironically, the Nazi military machine had belt buckles that boldly said "Gott mit uns" ("God is with us").[5]

This secular German philosophy taught that Jesus was not a Jew at all, but an Aryan, and that he didn't have a Jewish father. He was a warrior and a hero who died in the fight against Judaism. They even twisted Scripture to say that Jesus Himself called the entire Jewish race "children of the devil," and thus began the terrible purging of the Jews from Germany. This was done by "pastors" in pulpits and in schools in the guise of

---

4 During the signing of the Nazi-Vatican Concordat. See www.bee.net/cardigan/attic/120101.htm

5 See photo, "Was Hitler a Christian?": www.straightdope.com/mailbag/mhitlerchristian.html

the Christian faith. So tragically, in the eyes of many Jews, the evil of Nazism came directly through the Christian church.

As a result, when you and I approach a Jew with a New Testament in our hand, or a cross around our neck and sweetly say, "I would like to talk to you about Jesus," to them we may be saying, "Hi, I represent an institution that is filled with pedophiles, bows down to idols, worships false gods, and was responsible for the murder of six million Jews." No wonder they are reluctant to talk to us.

That's why when we talk to a Jew about God, we must start with Moses. He can understand that. Then we simply take them through the Ten Commandments to show them that they have sinned against God and that they desperately need a Savior. If their heart is humble, we should then unashamedly reveal the love of God displayed in the cross—that God Himself provided a Lamb for our atonement, and trust in His great faithfulness to bring them to everlasting life that is alone in Jesus Christ.

Started By Jews

Although Hollywood was started by Jews, it would seem that not too many of them could be considered orthodox (Jews who believed the Bible). They were more "liberal" rather than God-fearing. Marlon Brando said:

> "Hollywood was always a Jewish community; it was started by Jews and to this day is run largely by Jews. But for a long time it was venomously anti-Semitic in a perverse way, especially before the war, when Jewish performers had to disguise their Jewishness if they wanted a job. These actors were frightened, and understandably so. When I was breaking into acting, I constantly heard about agents submitting an actor or actress for a part, taking them to the theater for a reading and afterward hearing the producer say, 'Terrific. Thank you very much. We'll call you.'
>
> "After the actor was gone, the agent would ask, 'Well, Al, what did you think?'

"'Great,' the producer would say, 'He was terrific, but he's too Jewish.'

"If you 'looked Jewish,' you didn't get a part and couldn't make a living. You had to look like Kirk Douglas, Tony Curtis, Paul Muni or Paulette Goddard and change your name. They were Jews, but didn't 'look Jewish' and employed the camouflage of non-Jewish names."[6]

In an article entitled "Do Jews Run Hollywood?" Ben Stein[7] bounced off an inflammatory statement Marlon Brando made in a television interview:

"'Hollywood is run by Jews; it is owned by Jews—and they should have a greater sensitivity about the issue of people who are suffering. Because ... we have seen ... the greaseball, we've seen the Chink, we've seen the slit-eyed dangerous Jap, we have seen the wily Filipino, we've seen everything but we never saw the kike. Because they knew perfectly well, that that is where you draw the [line].' He [Brando] said that CBS's 60 Minutes called him and said that their research found that "only" about 60 percent of the most important positions in Hollywood were run by Jews. He [Brando] said, 'I managed to disqualify myself by saying that while Hollywood was not really "run" by anyone (it's far too chaotic for that), if Jews were about 2.5 percent of the population and were about 60 percent of Hollywood, they might well be said to be extremely predominant in that sector.'"[8]

As a Jew himself, Stein was offended by Brando's remarks, and said, "It was the Jews of the '30s and '40s who gave us the vision of America the Good, where money did not count—

---

6 Marlon Brando (with Robert Lindsey), *Brando: Songs My Mother Taught Me*, New York: Random House (1994), page 79.

7 Benjamin Jeremy Stein—an Emmy Award-nominated American lawyer, economist, law professor, actor, comedian, game show host and former White House speechwriter.

8 http://www.pass.to/newsletter/do_jews_run_hollywood.htm

only goodness. Think of the works of William Wyler (maker of the ultimate pro-American heartstrings movie, *The Best Years of Our Lives*), or of MGM and its celebration of the swinging good life of Ginger and Fred ... Where does the idea come from of the perfect American family, occasionally quarreling mildly but ultimately working it all out in love and affection? From *Ozzie and Harriet* and *Leave It to Beaver* and *I Love Lucy*, with their largely Jewish writers and producers."

Although Stein loves Hollywood, it is refreshing to hear his concern for the way the industry has gone in recent years. He said "Hollywood's current product occasionally repels and even sickens me. I am truly disgusted with its language, its violence, its endless attacks on businessmen and military officers."

Hollywood Jews and Jesus

When Goldie Hawn was questioned about her faith and whether her family had a Hebrew Bible or the Christian Bible in her home, she said, "We had the Old Testament and the New Testament." Her mom was Jewish and her dad a Presbyterian. She said:

"When you have a Jewish mother who has a very strong Jewish family, it's very ethnic in its practices. Eating brisket, the food and the family and the interconnectedness for better or worse. The intertwining of the family is a big part of the Jewish way of life. Whereas the Presbyterians are whiter. They don't have the same sense of family, although I have a very big and strong family on my dad's side. But it's not quite the same. It's like being Greek or Italian, you know what I mean, having this kind of ethnicity. So clearly my father's belief system was not wrapped around anything other than his own philosophical nature. He wasn't anyone who blindly had faith; he was a searcher, a seeker, and a philosopher.

"My best friend was Catholic and that also is a very strong pull. And because she was my best friend, I used to go to church with her all the time. "I also went to the Presbyterian church. And it was so great not to be stopped, you see. A parent can say, "You're Jewish, you don't get to do that. This is our faith, you don't get to learn about it." But my mother loved Jesus—she was just a complete Jesus freak … Oh, and I am too—that's another interesting thing.

"He went to the desert; he sat quietly. He sat so quietly that he heard the voice of God. He heard the truth. He felt the truth. He was able to receive the truth because he emptied himself and he had the ability to do it. Perhaps that was his specialness, or part of it.

"Because she [my mother] felt he was an extraordinary man. She didn't believe, of course, that he was the son of God. But she believed that he was one of the great humans, super humans, on the planet."[1]

Woody's Jewish Family

Woody Allen was born into a Jewish family, and he had the experience many youths have when it comes to the things of God. He said:

> "I was unmoved by the synagogue, I was not interested in the Seder, I was not interested in the Hebrew school, I was not interested in being Jewish," Woody says. "It just didn't mean a thing to me. I was not ashamed of it nor was I proud of it. It was a nonfactor to me. I didn't care about it. It just wasn't my field of interest. I cared about baseball, I cared about movies. To be a Jew was not something that I felt 'Oh, God, I'm so lucky.' Or 'Gee, I wish I were something else.' I certainly had no interest in being Catholic or in any of the other Gentile religions." The notion brings forth a laugh from him when he says it. "I thought those kids in Catholic school who couldn't see movies because the Legion of Decency wouldn't permit them, or who said their catechism, were silly beyond belief. I thought, 'What a waste of time.' And I felt the same thing in Hebrew school, my mind drifting out the window, not learning anything, just counting the minutes until it was over."[2]

---

1 http://www.beliefnet.com/story/172/story_17266_2.html

2 http://www.adherents.com/people/pa/Woody_Allen.html

Others in Hollywood have a measure of faith that spills out at the Oscars. It is God they thank for their success. They aren't ashamed to even mention Jesus in their speech. But a recurring theme is that most of these actors who have a measure of faith in Jesus stop at His exclusivity. They will speak of Him as a great teacher, or as their Lord, but they halt at His teachings about being the only way to God. They maintain that there are many paths to God, and Jesus is only one of them.

Tom Hanks

Tom Hanks became involved in a local church because he wasn't happy in his home life. He said "I mostly just wanted to get out of the house; the house wasn't a good place to be."

> The path Tom took was to religion. A club at school led him to the First Covenant Church, just down the hill at Skyline, and a faith that would dominate his life for the next four years.
>
> The church would provide friends, a girlfriend, structure, later even surrogate parents and a car. In return, the young recruit simply had to believe and to conform—two things born-again Tom was more than happy to do.
>
> Sister Sandra remembers her brother as being "self-righteous" around his Fundamentalist Christian period, "as if he had seen the light and the rest of us were in the dark."
>
> His father was equally dismissive, saying Tom suffered "an adolescent faith attack."
>
> He had already tried being a Catholic, a Mormon and a Nazarene. But those had always been forced on him by circumstance. Here was a religion that wanted him for himself, irrespective of who his mother happened to be.
>
> "Because of all the people I lived with, I had a checkered religious upbringing. Then, when I was in high school, I had a serious born-again experience," Tom explained in a *Los Angeles Times* interview. "A great group of people ran a church near where I lived, and they provided a safe,

nurturing atmosphere at a time there wasn't much else I could count on.

"The beliefs I embraced at that time don't mean the same thing to me now. When you're young and idealistic you tend to view things in absolute terms, and the absolutes didn't pan out, even within the confines of that place. You begin to see the contradictions without looking too closely."

It was a while though, before Tom started looking back to the secular world. For now, he was enjoying his own, contradictory rebellion. While other kids his age were straining at the leash, growing long hair, pubescent moustaches, playing truant from church, and testing authority, Tom was joining the congregation youth group and choir and faithfully attending both the morning and afternoon Sunday services at the Oakland church that had become his second home. In time, he wasn't just joining Bible readings, he was leading them.

He says he was "a Jesus freak," the sort of boy who would approach other students in the hallways at school and invite them to his house after class to discuss passages from the Bible. [He was 14 years old at the beginning of this period.][3]

Sylvester Stallone

Not many hit the silver screen the way Sylvester Stallone burst onto the scene. He didn't gain worldwide fame until his starring role in the smash hit *Rocky* (1976), the film was awarded the 1976 Academy Award for Best Picture. On March 24, 1975, Stallone saw the Ali-Chuck Wepner fight that inspired the foundation idea of *Rocky*. That night Stallone went home, and in three days he had written the script for *Rocky*. After that, he tried to sell the script with the intention of playing the lead role. Robert Chartoff and Irwin Winkler in particular liked the script (which was suggested by Stallone after a casting), and planned on courting a star like Burt Reynolds or James Caan for the lead role.

---

3 http://www.ldsfilm.com/actors/TomHanks.html

The final result was an unequalled success; *Rocky* was nominated for ten Academy Awards in all, including two for Stallone himself, for Best Actor and for Best Original Screenplay. In addition to winning Best Picture, *Rocky* won for Best Director and Best Film Editing. *Rocky* cost about US $1.1 million to make, and grossed about US $225 million worldwide. The sequel *Rocky II* was released in 1979 and also became a major success, grossing US $200 million worldwide

He said:

> "Anyone can shoot a pretty picture, but many people can't tell a story and move the heart. That is the key to longevity for a film. It must become part of them. It must be passionate and compelling in heart and energy. It can't just be car chases and fist fights; you must look at the message and the outcome. When you write from the heart, out comes a spiritual message."[4]

He has become philosophical when speaking of his success:

> "As a young person, you feel that the world revolves around you and that you have all the vim, vigor and energy to take on the world. But after you're knocked down a few times, you see that you need guidance, light and spiritual help. I now realize how heavily I rely upon Jesus, the Word of God and His support. I pass this lesson along to my kids, too ... that sometimes we have to learn things the hard way before it really takes hold. The more I listen to His Word and let Him guide my hand, the more He carries me. The more I turn myself over to the process of letting Him guide me, the more the pressure is off because He's carrying me."[5]

Madonna and Jesus

Madonna isn't Jewish, but as she matured, she threw herself into Jewish mysticism. In an interview with her about

---

4 http://www.christianlivingmag.com

5 http://www.christianlivingmag.com

her adopted son, Meredith Vieira (the interviewer) makes a very common mistake. She asks, "David, born a Christian. Will he be raised a Christian?"

However, no one has ever been "born a Christian." A Christian is someone who has repented and put his or her trust in Jesus Christ alone for eternal salvation. No doubt the interviewer was saying that the child was born in a "Christian" nation. Sadly, the word "Christian" is bandied about without much thought. It is sometimes used to describe us when we are fighting terrorists or the Catholic church, the Inquisitions, Crusades, etc. Despite this, Madonna knew what she meant and answered, "He's only you know thirteen months old. He's too young to have been indoctrinated into any kind of belief system. But if David decides he wants to be a Christian, then so be it." Meredith made reference to the fact that the child was holding "the red string, the Kabbalah." To which Madonna said:

> "I believe in Jesus
> and I study Kabbalah."
> –Madonna

> "But I believe in Jesus, and I study Kabbalah. So, I don't see why he can't too.
>
> "[People] don't know what Kabbalah is, and so they jump to conclusions. For me, studying Kabbalah is studying—is just—is asking questions. And I encourage all of my children to be that way, and I think people don't understand that. And so they make assumptions and they judge."[6]

When Madonna was accused of blasphemy by having herself put on a cross in one of her songs, she responded, "Of course some people thought, 'Oh, she's just being controversial, she's just getting on a cross and trying to [anger] people ...' but that wasn't my intention at all," she said. "Jesus' message was to love your neighbor as yourself, and there are people in need. I hope that people got that message," Madonna explained.

6 http://www.msnbc.msn.com/id/15518962/page/2/

Jesus is not the only figure the singer wants to model after. She further stated that she wants "to be like Gandhi and Martin Luther King and John Lennon."

"But I want to stay alive," she added.[7]

Steven Spielberg

Steven Spielberg once recalled, "I wasn't a religious kid, although I was Bar Mitzvahed in a real Orthodox synagogue."

In childhood, it's fair to say Steven Spielberg was a reluctant Jew. The theme of longing to belong permeated much of his work until only recently. It was only after fully accepting his Jewishness that Spielberg flowered as a mature artist, capable of producing his Oscar-winning masterpiece, *Schindler's List.*

"I wanted something that would confirm my Judaism to my family and myself, and to a history that was being forgotten. When my son was born, it greatly affected me. I decided I wanted my kids raised Jewish, as I was. I have wonderful memories of my Judaism when I was a child—not a teenager, but a child," he said, perhaps recalling the high school bullies who bloodied his nose ... "I wanted my children to be proud of the fact that they were members of the oldest tribe in history."

> "I wasn't a religious kid, although I was Bar Mitzvahed in a real Orthodox synagogue."
> —*Steven Spielberg*

Spielberg found belonging to the only Jewish family on the block a lonely position, especially at Christmas, when theirs was the sole house in the neighborhood unlit by decorations. In vain, the dying-to-assimilate youth begged his father to at least put a red light in the window. "I was ashamed because I was living on a street where at Christmas

---

7 Madonna: "We All Need to be Like Jesus," by Nathan Black, *Christian Post Reporter*, Feb. 16, 2007.

we were the only house with nothing but a porch light on," he has said.[8]

George Burns

George Burns was Jewish, but he didn't say too much about God. However, his whit revealed something: "The secret of a good sermon is to have a good beginning and a good ending, then having the two as close together as possible." He added, "The one issue that never came up between Gracie and me was religion. Gracie was a practicing Irish Catholic. She tried to go to Mass every Sunday. I was Jewish, but I was out of practice. My religion was always treat other people nicely and be ready when they play your music. Mary Kelly, who was also Irish Catholic, wouldn't marry Jack Benny because she didn't want to marry out of her faith, but Gracie didn't seem to care. In fact, I was a lot more concerned about what my mother thought than I was about Gracie."[9] It was said, as much as he looked forward to reaching age 100, George also stated that he looked forward to death, as the day he died he would be with Gracie again in Heaven.

Free Pass?

So, does the fact that I'm Jewish give me a free pass into heaven? In January 2000, a well-known ex-televangelist said on a worldwide TV talk show, "I believe that every person who died in the Holocaust went to heaven." He was very sincere, and if he was seeking the commendation of the world, he surely got it with that statement. Who wouldn't consider what he said to be utterly compassionate? However, let's look at the implications of his heartfelt beliefs. His statement seemed to limit salvation to the *Jews* who died in the Holocaust, because he added that "their blood laid a foundation for the nation

8 Frank Sanello, *Spielberg: The Man, the Movies, the Mythology*, Taylor Publishing Company: Dallas, Texas (1996).

9 George Burns, *Gracie: A Love Story*, G. P. Putnam's Sons: New York (1988), pages 64-65.

of Israel." If the slaughtered Jews made it to heaven, did the many *Gypsies* who died in the Holocaust also obtain eternal salvation? If his statement includes Gentiles, is the salvation he spoke of limited to those who died at the hands of Nazis? Did the many *Frenchmen* who met their death at the hands of cruel Nazis go to heaven also?

Perhaps he was saying that the death of Jesus on the cross covered *all* of humanity, and that all will eventually be saved—something called "universalism." This means that salvation will also come to Hitler and the Nazis who killed the Jews. However, I doubt if he was saying that. Such a statement would have brought the scorn of his Jewish host, and of the world whose compassion has definite limits. If pressed, he probably didn't mean that only the Jews in the camps went to heaven, because that smacks of *racism*. He was likely saying that those who died were saved because they died in such *tragic circumstances*. Then Jesus was lying when He said, "I am the way, the truth, and the life: no man comes to the Father, but by me" (John 14:6). There is another way to heaven—death in a Nazi concentration camp. Does that mean that the many Jews who died under *communism* went to heaven? Or is salvation limited to *German* concentration camps? If their salvation came because of the grim circumstances surrounding their death, does a Jew therefore enter heaven after suffering for hours before dying in a car wreck ... if he was killed by a drunk driver who happened to be German? Bear in mind that his suffering may have been much greater than someone who died within minutes in a Nazi gas chamber.

Many unsaved people think we *can* merit entrance into heaven by our suffering. Their error was confirmed by this sincere, compassionate man of God. They may now disregard the truth, "Neither is there salvation in any other: for there is no other name under heaven given among men, whereby we must be saved" (Acts 4:12). They can now save themselves by the means of their own death ... if they suffer enough.

The ex-televangelist was concerned that his indiscretions of the 1980s brought discredit to the kingdom of God. However, those actions fade into history compared to the damage done by saying that there is another means of salvation outside of Jesus Christ, on a program watched by untold millions around the world. Who on earth needs to repent and trust in Jesus, if millions entered the kingdom without being born again? No one.

The Connection

Let me assume that you are a Christian or at least you have some sort of faith in God, and that you have a genuine desire to please Him. It's with that supposition that I want to address what I believe is the answer to the Hollywood dilemma.

The reason Hollywood is so successful in pumping out its filth is because there is a thirsty market for it. The only way to dry up the market is for God to change people's hearts through the power of the gospel.

Before I began itinerating many years ago, I was a pastor at a local church in New Zealand. It was good for me to experience three and a half years of tribulation before I stepped into other men's pulpits. It meant that I could empathize with them about the hassles of pastoring a local church ... and there *are* hassles. There are complicated marital problems, those who fall into adultery, pornography, and other sexual vices. Then there are the complainers, the backbiters, those who cause division, and the ones that sneak into the church with weird doctrines. Add to that the concerns of having the sick who need visiting, weddings to perform, funerals to undertake, Sunday schools to run, board meetings to attend, messages to prepare, and the care of his own family, and no wonder so many pastors suffer from burn out.[1]

---

1 "Peacemaker Ministries" report that every month, 1,500 pastors in the USA leave their assignments because of conflict, burnout or moral failure. www.peacemaker.net.

The problem with many of our churches is that we have unwittingly replaced the narrow gate with a broad path, and this has filled our pews with tares that sit among the wheat. The garden of the average local church is so filled with weeds they are choking healthy growth, and all the extra work they are causing is wearing out the gardener.

The Three Principles

The way we can get a healthy church is to make sure that we do all we can to ensure that we see *genuine* converts. These people undergird the church financially. They support the pastor prayerfully, have an all-consuming fire for the lost,[2] are zealous prayer warriors who live holy lives and have good sound doctrine. They thirst after righteousness and keep their hearts free from sin because they know that they are called to deny themselves and take up the cross daily. In other words, the local church becomes filled with normal biblical Christians.

The *Book of Exodus* gives us three principles that will help to make this a reality. But before we look at them, let me tell you about an interesting incident that happened recently at our ministry.

I was sitting in our editing suite when Anita, a member of our staff, popped her head in the door and said, "Kevin wants to see you." When she saw that I had no idea what "Kevin" she was talking about, she said, "You know ... *Kevin*. The drug addict." "Oh, *that* Kevin. Tell Danny to get some money and buy him lunch ... if that's what he wants."

Kevin was a mess. He looked sick. Deathly sick. He had destroyed his liver through drug abuse and doctors had tried to compensate for it by implanting three or four devices the size of small golf balls under the skin of his upper right arm. It looked horrible. I would often see him stumbling around the neighborhood and it seemed that it would be just a matter of time until we would find his body lying on the sidewalk.

---

2 Charles Spurgeon said, "Have you no wish for others to be saved? Then you are not saved yourself. Be sure of that."

I felt sorry for Kevin, so I told him that if he was ever hungry, he was to drop into the ministry, and I would get him some food. Every couple of months he would show up, and I would have someone take him to lunch.

I had tried to witness to him, but he became so angry I backed off. All I could do was love him in some tangible way. He was now back, and no doubt hungry.

After I told Anita what to do, I noticed that my wife had done what I asked her to do the night before. She had moved two tablets with the Ten Commandments on them into the lobby, just outside the editing suite. Someone had sent them to me as a gift a year or so earlier. Up until the day before, they had been sitting in our store, but for some reason I decided to have them put in a prominent place in the lobby.

A few minutes later, as I walked through our store I bumped into Kevin. "Danny will be here in a minute." He looked at me and said, "I want to see *you*."

I sat down beside him and noticed that he reeked of marijuana. "I have a fine. If I don't pay it I will have to go to prison. If you could help out by paying part of it …" I asked how much it was. "It's quite a bit—180 dollars." He opened his wallet and pulled out some court paperwork. I took it, told him that I would see what I could do, and left him sitting in the store.

A moment later I was in the office of our Chief Financial Officer asking if we could legally pay Kevin's fine. His facial expression revealed that he was a little reticent to pay the fine of someone who was on drugs, but he kindly wrote a check made out to the local courts and gave it to me.

As I walked back into the store I handed it to Kevin and said, "I really care about you Kevin." He stared at it and said, "This is *such* a relief. *I don't have to go to prison.* Thank you!"

Then I said, "Come with me," and I took him upstairs to meet our CFO. Kevin thanked Ron and said that the last time he was in court, the judge didn't even look up at him. He just looked at some paperwork and sent him to prison for three days.

On the way back to the store, we stopped in the lobby in front of the Ten Commandments. I pointed at them and said, "That's the Law *I* broke Kevin." He leaned down to focus on them and said, "The Ten Commandments ..." I then said, "But Jesus paid my fine, and now I don't have to go to Hell."

He went quiet for a moment and quietly said, "I'm beginning to see the connection." As we stopped at the door he looked me in the eyes and said, "I *really* appreciate this. If there is ever *anything* I can do for you, please tell me."

His words echoed in my mind. "*I'm beginning to see the connection.*" It was the knowledge that I had broken the Ten Commandments that helped him to make a connection to the payment of the cross. After all, a fine being paid has no meaning if there is no knowledge that a law has been broken.

It's Not Enough

Let's now look at those three principles. The *Book of Exodus* tells us that after the famous burning bush incident, God told Moses that He would use him to deliver Israel from the bondage of Egypt. Then Moses asked who he should say sent him:

> "And God said to Moses, I AM THAT I AM: and he said, Thus shall you say to the children of Israel, I AM has sent me to you" (Exodus 3:14).

God then gave him some details about what would happen when he went to Egypt, but despite this incredible encouragement, Moses insisted that his hearers wouldn't believe that he was speaking for God. He wanted something more:

> "And Moses answered and said, But, behold, they will not believe me, nor hearken to my voice: for they will say, The LORD has not appeared to you. And the LORD said

to him, What is that in your hand? And he said, A rod"
(Exodus 4:1-2).

Moses was holding a rod that God said he was to cast to
the ground.[3] Perhaps he had thought that his rod could only
be used to fend off wild beasts. But when he did what God
told him to do, it became something completely different. It
turned into a serpent from which Moses understandably fled.
Then God told him to reach out and take it by the tail. He did
so, and it turned back to being his rod. This was to be a "sign"
that God had sent him.

Moses was then given a second sign that would help to
convince his hearers that he was a spokesman for God. He
was told to put his hand into his breast and take it out. When
he did so "his hand was as leprous as snow" (Exodus 4:6). He
was instructed to repeat the process and this time his hand
was clean of the disease. These two signs were given for the
purpose of convincing his hearers that he was sent from God
to speak to them.

But there was one more sign Moses could fall back on if
they still didn't believe that God was speaking through him.
He was to take water out of the Nile and pour it upon the dry
land. When he did this, the water would turn into blood.

So here are the three signs he was given, to make his
hearers believe that the message Moses had was from God.
He was to:

1. Cast the rod down and it would become a serpent.

2. Put his hand into his breast and it would become leprous,
then become clean again.

3. Pour water onto the ground and it would become
blood.

---

3 The shepherd's rod was used to fend off wild beasts. It was his most
precious possession. He would take much time selecting a suitable tree and
a branch without knots, a piece of wood which was strong and straight, and
he would spend weeks carving and smoothing it. It would never leave his
side; it was his entrusted weapon.

I can understand why Moses reacted as he did. When I speak to the lost, I want more than "God sent me to tell you something." The world is full of people who say that they were sent by God. Jehovah's Witnesses say that they are His representatives on earth. I AM sent them. So do Mormons. They say that they represent God. Muslims say a similar thing; and there are a myriad of cults, strange sects and weirdos who say that they are speaking for God.

We will now look at three "signs" that separate the true Church from the "God sent me" folks. They will help to convince an unbelieving world that the message we have is truly heaven-sent.

The Question

Let me ask you the same question that God asked Moses— "What is that in your hand?" It is the rod of Moses. Perhaps you didn't give any thought to the fact that you have it in your hand to do as you please. You do *hold* to the Law, don't you? Do you think that it is good? Is it right for the Law to forbid murder, stealing, lying and adultery? Of course you hold to it. We cannot fault the Moral Law. As the Bible says, it is perfect, holy, just and good.[4] Perhaps you've never really thought much about the Ten Commandments or of the fact that you could do anything evangelistic with them. You have simply used them to steady yourself morally in your Christian walk, and to fend off the enemy's attacks. You know that to transgress any of the Law's precepts—to lie, or covet, or steal, or commit adultery is to "give place to the devil."

But, as you study Scripture, you will see that the Law can be turned into something radically different. It can be used to bring to this world "the knowledge of sin."[5] It can be used as a "schoolmaster" to bring sinners to Christ.[6] Jesus, Paul and

---

4 See Psalm 19:7 and Romans 7:12.

5 See Romans 3:20.

6 See Galatians 3:24.

others cast it down to be a serpent to guilty sinners—to be a convincing sign that God had sent them.[7]

So, do what Moses did. Simply cast it down before the feet of a sinful world and watch what it does. In this case, seeing *is* believing. The Law bites into the human conscience. It has power to kill. This is what it did for Paul in his own life. In Romans 7:7 he explained how the Law showed him the true nature of sin—that it was *exceedingly* sinful. It produced evidence of his guilt and then it passed its terrible sentence. The Law condemned him to death. With Paul, the serpent had a *fatal* bite:

> "For I was alive without the law once: but when the commandment came, sin revived, and I died. And the commandment, which was ordained to life, I found to be unto death" (Romans 7:9-10).

The Law of God plagues a guilty sinner in the same way civil law plagues a guilty criminal. A murderer has little concern if he thinks that he has outwitted the law. But the moment it puts steal handcuffs on his wrists, it produces a justifiable fear. It arrests him and forces him to the just retribution of the hangman's noose.

That's why we mustn't allow the world to think for a moment that it has outwitted God's Law. They must be made to understand that the Judge of the Universe will bring *every* work to judgment, including every secret thing, whether it is good or evil.[8] And the way to convince them that what you are saying is true, is to simply cast the rod at their feet. That's all you have to do. God will do the rest. He will do a miracle by making the dead inanimate rod of the Law, a living and fiery serpent.[9]

---

7 See *What Did Jesus Do?* By Ray Comfort.

8 See Ecclesiastes 12:14.

9 See John 16:8.

You Need Not Fear

The Scriptures tell us that the serpent terrified Moses, so that he "fled from before it." That's what the average Christian tends to do with the Law. We tend to keep away from it. It's a little scary. But God said to Moses, "Put forth your hand and take it by the tail" (Exodus 4:4), and when he did that, it returned to being a rod in his hand.

If you are a Christian, you don't need to dread the Law. You can take it by the tail. You are in Christ, so the Law will not bite you.[10] Moses cannot enter the Promised Land of the Gospel. All he can do is take you there. The moment the Law has acted as a schoolmaster to bring you to Christ, his job is done.[11] So take hold of it and do what Jesus did.[12] Let the world know that lust is adultery in God's sight.[13] Tell them that a holy God considers hatred to be murder.[14] Use the Ten Commandments as Paul did when he personalized them for his hearers. He said, "You who say, 'You shall not steal,' do *you* steal? You who say 'You shall not commit adultery,' do *you* commit adultery? You that abhor idols, do *you* commit sacrilege?" (Romans 2:21-22, italics added).

When we cast down the rod of the Law, it helps to convince them that the gospel of salvation is from God. Once they are "convinced of the Law as transgressors,"[15] they are ready for the good news of the gospel—that they can be saved from its bite because the rod has already struck the Savior for our justification. The Law's holy demands have been satisfied in Christ. In Exodus 17:5, when Moses *used his rod* to strike a rock, water gushed out. The New Testament tells us that "Christ was that rock" (1 Corinthians 10:4). Jesus had to be

---

10 See Romans 8:1.

11 Deuteronomy 4:22; Galatians 3:24.

12 See Mark 10:17.

13 Matthew 5:27-28.

14 See 1 John 3:15.

15 James 2:9.

struck by Moses before we could freely drink of the water of life.[16]

Why the Law Convinces

So how then does the rod of the Law convince an unbelieving world that the message that you have for them is from "I AM"? It persuades *because it reveals a terrible dilemma that only the gospel can address.*

Think of it like this. I offer you four gifts:

1. An expensive painting.
2. A brand new car.
3. A year's supply of groceries.
4. A parachute.

You can only take one. Which would you choose? Before you make your choice, here's some information that will help to persuade you as to which one is the best choice: *you have to jump 10,000 feet out of a plane.*

That *does* help you to connect the dots. You *need* the parachute because it's the only one of the four gifts that will help with your dilemma. The others may have some use, but they are useless when it comes to facing the law of gravity from a 10,000 foot fall.

Think now of the four great religions: Hinduism, Buddhism, Islam, and Christianity. Which should Hollywood and the rest of the world choose? If you leave the Law of God out of the equation (and its terrifying wrath for transgression), it doesn't really matter which one is chosen. Without knowledge of the Law, man is considered to have his faults but he's basically good at heart. So, as long as he is sincere in his religion it doesn't matter to which one he belongs. God is merciful and kind, and therefore forgiving. So the sincere devotee to any religion will more than likely make it to heaven. How could he not?

---

16 See John 7:37-38.

But bring the Law in and show that a holy Creator has a perfect Law that deems lust to be adultery, hatred to be murder, and warns that all liars will have their part in the lake of fire, and the equation radically changes. The fact that God's wrath abides upon the sinner cuts down his options.[17]

Hinduism can't help. It says that the sinner goes through the door of death and hopefully he will come back as some other creature. It doesn't deal with the problem of sin and wrath.

Buddhism can't help. It denies God and His justice, and says that the door is an illusion. It doesn't deal with our sin and wrath problem.

Islam can't help. It acknowledges sin, but hopes that God will extend His mercy towards sinners … if they are repentant, pray regularly, and fast. He will see their religious works *and because of them* show mercy. They lack understanding of the true nature of the Law, and therefore they don't see that they are guilty criminals standing before a holy Judge. Their religious works therefore are an attempt to bribe the Judge of the Universe. The Bible says that *because of our guilt*, anything we offer God for our justification is an abomination to Him.[18] Islam makes no provision to deal with our problem of sin and wrath.

However, in Christianity, God Himself provided a "Savior"—a parachute, and the Bible tells us exactly what to do. It says "Put on the Lord Jesus Christ." Jesus of Nazareth on a bloodied cross deals perfectly with our terrible dilemma. Christianity provides a perfect Savior from the Law's wrath against our sin, *and at the same time convinces your hearers that you are speaking for God.*

Think of it. You are standing on the edge of a 10,000 foot drop. You are going to die! Terror fills your heart. Why?

---

17 See John 3:36.

18 See Proverbs 15:8.

Because you know that the law of gravity is a harsh reality, and it will therefore kill you.

Suddenly someone offers you a beautiful painting. You ignore it. Another passes you the keys to a brand new car. Someone else puts a grocery voucher into your hand. You let them both drop to the floor of the plane, and stand there in horror at your impending fate. Suddenly, someone says, "Here's a parachute!" *Which one of the four people is going to hold the most credibility in your eyes?* To which person will you pay attention? You shouldn't have to give it too much thought.

The Law pins us to the cross as surely as Roman law pinned the penitent thief to the cross. His case was over. He was utterly helpless and his future was hopeless. He couldn't go anywhere, he couldn't do anything. All he could do was turn his face to Jesus and ask for mercy.

The Law helps your hearers make the connection between their dilemma and the solution. It gives you and your message of salvation credibility. Once the connection is made, it shows the world that "I AM" has sent you. They have violated the Law, and the Gospel has the answer. It has the *only* answer. It makes the exclusivity of the Savior make sense. This is why so many popular preachers (who never reference the Law and its wrath) vacillate when it comes to Jesus being the *only* way to God. Again, if you leave out the Law, you will leave your hearers with the delusion that they are basically good at heart and therefore don't need a Savior. If there is no knowledge of wrath, there is no need of mercy. In the next chapter, we will look at the root of man's problem.

What's the Problem?

Man's predicament isn't intellectual. It's *moral*. All sane men know intellectually that God exists. This is why Hollywood has so few atheists. Most are anti-God, but as intelligent people they could never say, in the face of creation and with the voice of conscience, that there is no God. The Bible tells us that when it comes to having a knowledge of whether or not there is a Creator "they are without excuse" (see Romans 1:18-20). But if we remove the Law from the evangelistic equation we eclipse his moral problem and *make* it intellectual.

If we don't reference the law, the perception becomes that the criminal is no longer a criminal. Instead, he is an unfortunate man who finds himself in a courtroom, and he's struggling to know if the courtroom had a builder, or if it was built over a long period of time, or if the judge really exists, etc.

It is because the Law has been forsaken in evangelism that we have entire ministries built solely on arguments meant to convince sinners that God exists, that the Bible is His Word and that our origins are in Him. I *love* apologetics and use them regularly when preaching to the lost.[1] Yet the truth is, if God wanted to merely convince an unbelieving world intellectually that the Bible is His Word, all He needed to do was include a few chapters that speak clearly about how to

---

1 See, *The Evidence Bible*, which is packed full of apologetics.

invent the internal combustion engine, how to build a plane that flies, how to make a television set that works, how to invent the telephone, the computer, the remote control and a few other conveniences He knew that we would struggle to invent thousands of years later. Divine inspiration of the Scriptures would then be undeniable.

The same applies with Messianic prophecy. Why didn't Isaiah clearly say, "Here are the signs of the Messiah so that you won't miss Him: "His name will be Jesus of Nazareth. His mother will be Mary and his earthy father will be Joseph the son of Heli. He will be born to a virgin in Bethlehem, be raised in Nazareth, do incredible miracles, be crucified by the Romans and then rise from death on the third day." But instead, Messianic prophecy is *hidden* in Scripture, and even when you find it, it's open to interpretation. If you don't believe that, take your best Messianic verses and share them with a Jew who knows the Scriptures. He will more than likely disarm you within two minutes. He will shoot holes in your favorite passages and make your evangelistic heart sink. For example, did you know that Psalm 22:16 is open to interpretation as to whether or not the wording says they "pierced my hands and my feet"? A common interpretation is, "For dogs have surrounded me; a band of evildoers encompassed me; like a lion *[they are at]* my hands and my feet."[2]

And even the number one favorite evangelistic passage of Messianic Scripture, Isaiah 53, will more than likely be interpreted by a Jew as being national Israel. It is obviously speaking about Jesus. However, if the reader of the chapter is prejudiced against Jesus, he will want to make it read as national Israel, rather than be a suffering individual. As we have seen, there is a reason for much of the prejudice in that Hitler used the New Testament to justify the holocaust.

You must be aware that the secular media annually gives prime time national television to show the pope bowing to

---

idols at Christmas and Easter. To the Jew, the pope represents Christianity. So the Jew equates Jesus of Nazareth with Nazi Germany and an idolatrous religious system that is filled with pedophiles. Understandably, a good Jew is going to have a strong prejudice against anything that his own religion tells him is an abomination to his God.[3]

Evolutionary Unreasonableness

A sin-loving and contentious evolutionist can also stump an evangelistic Christian who stays in the intellect and never moves to the conscience. All he has to do is be *unreasonable.* And he has a great reason to be unreasonable. Most ardent evolutionists have a hidden agenda.

The author Aldous Huxley, a member of one of England's intellectually distinguished families (whose grandfather, Thomas Huxley, was "Darwin's Bulldog" who championed Darwin's theory of evolution) admitted:

> "For myself, as, no doubt, for most of my contemporaries, the philosophy of meaninglessness was essentially an instrument of liberation. The liberation we desired was simultaneously liberation from a certain political and economic system *and liberation from a certain system of morality. We objected to the morality because it interfered with our sexual freedom.* There was one admirably simple method of confuting these people and at the same time

---

3 "If Isaiah 53 was referring to Jesus, why was Peter surprised to learn that Jesus would suffer? Matthew, in 16:21-22, wrote 'From that time forth began Jesus to show to his disciples that he must go to Jerusalem ... and suffer and be killed ... Then Peter took him, and began to rebuke him saying, 'Be it far from you, Lord: this shall not be to you.' Peter would have known after all, they built a church in his name and the first Pope was named Peter. Peter would have said, 'Hurray, prophesy is being fulfilled!' But, he didn't. Therefore, any discussion on Isaiah 53 is meaningless from a Christian position. The ONLY valid meaning is that of the original Hebrew." (From a Jewish website--http://jdstone.org/cr/index.html).

justifying ourselves in our political and erotic revolt: We could deny that the world had any meaning whatsoever."[4]

In other words, if evolution is true, the world has no meaning. There is therefore no God who demands moral accountability. That means fornication is okay. So is pornography, lust, and adultery.

Mr. Huxley spoke biblical truth. Romans 8:7 reveals that the hostility that the "carnal mind" (the intellect) has is directed at the Law of God. Again, the human mind gravitates towards the meaninglessness of evolution because it liberates from the requirements of the Moral Law. Darwinism switches out the light of accountability.

It is because apologetical argument is limited to the intellect that it should only be seen as a means to an end. That "end" is for them to receive a knowledge of sin so that they will see their need of a Savior. The only biblical way to do this is to address the conscience.

David's Sexual Freedom

Nothing had interfered with the sexual freedom King David had with his neighbor's wife. But his adultery had left a problem. His "tango" had left his partner pregnant. So he simply had her husband murdered, took her as his own, and moved on with life. He had all the bases covered.[5]

Nathan's agenda was to strike him out. So he didn't stay for too long in the king's intellect. He didn't talk of a wonderful plan, or of a God-shaped vacuum in his heart. He didn't play music, dim the lights or ask the king to close his eyes and bow his head. His sin had to be exposed if he was to find mercy and be saved from wrath. Nathan said, "Why have you despised the commandment of the Lord?" He quickly cast the rod down at his feet, and David was fatally smitten.[6]

---

4 *Ends and Means*, 1946, p. 270 (italics added).

5 See 2 Samuel 12.

6 2 Samuel 12:9-13.

"But," you say, "things are different nowadays. We have serious intellectual issues of which Nathan didn't have to deal. We have the theory of Darwinian evolution and rampant atheism, moral relativism, and widespread intellectual skepticism."

These issues are merely smoke screens of minds that are hostile to the Law of God. You need to simply clear the smoke. *What is that in your hand?* Cast it down at their feet.

We receive many emails and calls from Christians (who have grown weary in battle) who have incorporated the Law into their evangelism and they have been greatly encouraged. It did for them what the sweetness of honey did for a battle-weary Jonathan after he dipped forth *the end of the rod that was in his hand* into a honeycomb. His eyes were "enlightened" (see 1 Samuel 14:27).

Cast the Law down. Incorporate it into your gospel presentation and you will have your eyes enlightened. You will be *greatly* encouraged.

If we don't use what God has given us, and instead make the world believe through other means, we should understand the consequences.[7] If we convert a man to intellectually accept the gospel, *and there's no biblical knowledge of sin*, the man is not saved. He may make a "decision" in reference to Jesus and His death on the cross, but he will then sit among God's people as a tare among the wheat, until God sorts out the true from the false on the Day of Wrath. It is because of unbiblical evangelism methods that our churches are tragically filled with such people.

So the first thing Moses was to do, so that his hearers would believe that God had sent him, was to cast down his rod. We will look at the other two principles in the next chapter.

---

7 "Ignorance of the nature and design of the Law is at the bottom of most religious mistakes." John Newton. Charles Spurgeon said, "I do not believe that any man can preach the gospel who does not preach the Law."

The Leprous Hand

We are learning how we can convince an unbelieving world that the message that we have for them is directly from God by looking at three things that God said to Moses.

The *second* thing that Moses was to do to convince his hearers that his message was divine was to put his hand into his breast and take it out to reveal that it was leprous. He was to repeat the process, and it would be clean.

That should be the normal Christian's testimony. When we were confronted by God's demand for perfection, we had the personal revelation that our heart was filthy with the hopeless disease of sin.[1] We were then given clean hands and a pure heart by the grace of God.[2] Righteousness was imputed to us through the blood of the cross—we were freely given the righteousness of Christ. He justified us, washed us, and made it as though we had never sinned at all. Every Christian should have that testimony.

You have thrown down the rod of the Law. You hearer has become wide-eyed but he's not alarmed about his state. What are you to do? You put your hand into your breast and reveal your personal leprosy. Tell him about your personal sin and the reality of your redemption. Help him further to connect the Law he has violated with the mercy of the gospel. That's

---

1 See Ephesians 2:12.

2 See Psalm 24:3,4.

all I did with Kevin the drug addict. I pointed to the Law that revealed my leprous sin, and then to the Savior who cleansed me. That was what made him say, "I'm beginning to make the connection."

So the second means by which the sinner is helped to believe that the message you have is from God is your personal testimony—your heart was unclean, and now you are forgiven through the cleansing power of the gospel.

"The River of Pleasure"

Here now is the third principle that God gave to Moses to help his hearers believe that "I AM" had sent him. If they would not believe the first two signs, he was to take water from the river and pour it onto the ground. The water would then turn into blood.

What can you say to someone who hears the Law, and then hears your personal testimony, but still remains complacent? Look at 2 Timothy 4:2 (*Amplified* Bible):

> "Herald and preach the Word! Keep your sense of urgency [stand by, be at hand and ready], whether the opportunity seems to be favorable or unfavorable. [Whether it is convenient or inconvenient, whether it is welcome or unwelcome, you as preacher of the Word are to show people in what way their lives are wrong.] And convince them, rebuking and correcting, warning and urging and encouraging them, being unflagging and inexhaustible in patience and teaching."

If you love him you will *have* to rebuke him. This takes a little extra courage, but you must gently tell him that the day will come when the river of pleasure from which he drinks will dry up. It will turn to thick and cold blood in his mouth. The pleasures of sin are only for a season. The first sips may be sweet and satisfying to the taste, but they will bring the bitterness of death and everlasting damnation to those who continue to drink.

If someone I am speaking to is complacent, I often say, "If your eyes and my eyes meet on the Day of Judgment, and you are still in your sins, I am free from your blood. I have told you the truth. Your blood will be upon your own head. You will have no one to blame but yourself. Please give this deep and serious thought. You could die tonight, and there's no second chance. Thanks for listening. Nice to meet you ..."

These may seem like hard words, but they are soft and tender compared to the terror of the Lake of Fire. I am aghast beyond words at the fate of the lost. Paul said, "Wherefore *knowing the terror of the Lord*, we persuade men." So few know the terror of the Lord. So few believe that it is a fearful thing to fall into the hands of the Living God. We forget that sin has stored up heaven's wrath, and the Day will come when it is revealed.[3] The wooden rod of Moses will become an unbending rod of iron in the hand of a wrath-filled and Almighty God:

> "And out of his mouth goes a sharp sword, that with it he should smite the nations: and he shall rule them with a rod of iron: and he treads the winepress of the fierceness and wrath of Almighty God" (Revelation 19:15).

All humanity, including blasphemous Hollywood who so despised His precious name, will bow the knee to Jesus Christ as Lord, and Judge of the Universe:

> "Wherefore God also has highly exalted him, and given him a name which is above every name: That at the name of Jesus every knee should bow, of things in heaven, and things in earth, and things under the earth; And that every tongue should confess that Jesus Christ is Lord, to the glory of God the Father" (Philippians 2:9-11).

---

3 See Romans 2:4-12.

The Bottom Line

If you read through each confrontation Moses had with Pharaoh, you will see him lift his rod to bring in the plagues. That's what the Law does. It issues ten terrible plagues upon the hard-hearted. It helps them to see that God Himself delivered up His Firstborn, so that they could go free.

The rod of Moses was also lifted to open the Rea Sea so that Israel could be delivered from the hand of the enemy (see Exodus 14:16). The Law makes sinners "stand still." It helps them to see the salvation of God.

Each of us can take the same rod and see it produce fruit. When Moses went into the Tabernacle of Witness, it was Aaron's rod that budded (see Numbers 17:8). That was an unbelieving Israel's proof that he was speaking for God. It convinced them that "I AM" had sent him.

Incorporate the Law into your tabernacle of witness and watch the Gospel blossom to life.

We hear sermons about Aaron and Hur holding up the hands of Moses, as Joshua fought Amalek. As long as his hands were held up, Joshua succeeded in battle. Look at what Moses was holding:

> "And Moses said to Joshua, Choose us out men, and go out, fight with Amalek: tomorrow I will stand on top of the hill *with the rod of God in my hand*" (Exodus17:9, italics added).

The enemy hates this teaching because he knows that when we lift up the rod of the Law we will prevail. Scripture and church history testify to that.[4] He knows that if our evangelistic efforts (with the help of God) produce genuine

---

4 The Assistant Superintendent of a major U.S. denomination stated: "In the last ten years (1996 through 2005), we had 5.3 million stated decisions for Christ. The growth of our Sunday a.m. service during that period was only 221,890. That is only 4.2 percent conversion growth." See *The Way of the Master* for more of these little known statistics that reveal the results of modern evangelism.

converts, they will in turn reproduce of their own kind, set our churches on fire and bring revival to this dying world.

Look to the Future

So here's the bottom line. Does your faith or your religion deal with your problem of God's anger against your sin? Or is it like so many of those in the entertainment industry? If it's mere principles of self help, it's going to leave you in your sins … and if eternal and uncompromising justice finds you out on Judgment Day, your sins will take you to Hell.

When Jesus was first born the angel said, "He shall save His people *from their sins*." That's what we need—saving from the consequences of our own sins—not a self help religion that leaves us in sin.

Madonna said, "I want to stay alive." Who in his or her right mind doesn't? However, so few, especially in proud and blasphemous Hollywood, take that statement and humbly whisper it to God. He alone has immortality, and those who come to Him sincerely seeking truth will end up at the foot of the cross … whether Jew or Gentile.

It was a typically tongue-in-cheek cigar-smoking George Burns who said, "I look to the future because that's where I'm going to spend the rest of my life." He was right. He did spend his future here on earth, until it ran out at the age of one hundred years. He would have been better to say, "I look to the future because that's where I'm going to spend the rest of my *eternity*."

There are only a few actors whose names have been etched into the stone of immortality. They are the ones Hollywood calls "immortals." At one time in our history they gained the love and attention of the whole world, but even stone crumbles in time. Most of them are now faded stars, hardly visible to the naked eyes of a new generation. We already have youth that are instantly bored by slow-moving black and white movies. If asked who "John Wayne" is, they would probably reply, "Isn't that an airport in California?"

There is only one place that our names will be of *eternal* consequence. That is, if they are written in the Lamb's Book of Life. Will your name be there?

Think of the words of Marilyn Monroe:

> "Hollywood's a place where they'll pay you a thousand dollars for a kiss, and fifty cents for your soul."

Then think of the words of Jesus of Nazareth and what He paid for your soul to be saved:

> "What shall it profit a man, if he shall gain the whole world, and lose his own soul?"[5]

---

5 Mark 8:36

For a complete list of books, tracts, DVDs and audios by
Ray Comfort go to www.livingwaters.com

Also, tune into "The Way of the Master Radio" at
www.WayOfTheMasterRadio.com

Make sure you visit www.HollywoodandGod.com
to see powerful video clips and a list of contemporary
movies that use blasphemy.

"The Way of the Master"
Evidence Bible

Prove God's existence. Answer 100 common objections to Christianity. Show the Bible's supernatural origin. This unique study Bible includes wisdom from the foremost Christian leaders of yesterday and today such as Charles Spurgeon, D.L. Moody, John Wesley, Charles Finney, George Whitefield, Billy Graham, Dr. Bill Bright, John MacArthur, and R.C. Sproul.

Complete Bible available in
• Hardback
• Leather-bound (black or burgundy)
• Paperback

New Testament, Proverbs & Pslams
   available in
• Paperback
• Black leather-bound pocket editon

AVAILABLE AT FINE CHRISTIAN BOOKSTORES

Bridge-Logos Titles from Ray Comfort to Help You Share Your Faith

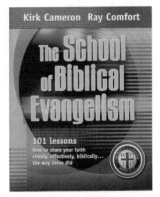

The School of Biblical Evangelism
In this comprehensive study course, you will learn how to share your faith simply, effectively, and biblically—the way Jesus did. Discover the God-given evangelistic tools that will enable you to confidently talk about the Savior.

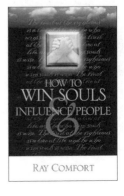

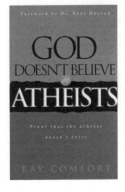

More **Bridge-Logos** Titles
from Ray Comfort

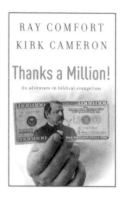

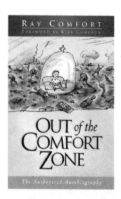

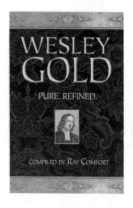

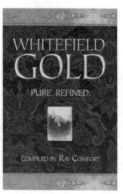

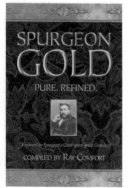